GASLIGHTING

HOW TO RECOGNIZE MANIPULATIVE AND EMOTIONALLY ABUSIVE PEOPLE WHILE RECOVER FROM A TOXIC RELATIONSHIP, AVOID BORDERLINE PERSONALITIES AND GET FREE FROM NARCISSIST'S FAVORITE TOOL

Julie A.Gift

Table of Contents

INTRODUCTION 4

CHAPTER 1.   BORDERLINE PERSONALITY 5

WHAT IS A BORDERLINE PERSONALITY 5

WHAT CAUSES A BORDERLINE PERSONALITY DISORDER 13

SYMPTOMS OF BORDERLINE PERSONALITY DISORDER 18

THERAPIES FOR BORDERLINE PERSONALITY DISORDERS 30

CHAPTER 2.   GASLIGHTING 49

WHAT IS GASLIGHTING? 49

HOW NARCISSISTS CONTROL YOU 55

EFFECTS OF GASLIGHTING 66

GASLIGHTING AT WORKPLACE 76

GASLIGHTING IN THE HOME 77

GASLIGHTING IN SOCIETY 79

CHAPTER 3.   TOXIC RELATIONSHIPS RECOVERY 81

HOW TO REDUCE CONFLICTS IN RELATIONSHIPS 81

HOW TO RECOGNIZE MANIPULATION AND TAKE BACK CONTROL 94

OVERCOMING LONELINESS 96

CHOOSING A NEW PARTNER 99

CREATING A HEALTHY RELATIONSHIP 105

HOW TO DEAL WITH A PERSON WITH A BORDER PERSONALITY DISORDER 108

CONCLUSION 122

Introduction

You have no doubt heard of gaslighting as it is has been publicized quite a lot over the last few years.

Put simply gaslighting is a form of psychological and emotional abuse and it causes the victim to second guess everything and question their own sanity. In this case, the person will not know whether to trust their own thoughts or actions or not and will often side-step the advice from their friends and family, simply because they feel so uncertain.There is no accurate way to explain how gaslighting feels. It is a constant feeling of uncertainty, enough to cause you to think you're going insane. Put simply, it's severe, whether the gaslighting is used mildly or not.

If you look for a definition of gaslighting you will see a description along the lines of:

"A form of psychological and emotional manipulation, when a person sows the seeds of doubt into their victim, causing them to question their thoughts, memory, sanity, and perception".

All types of narcissists can and do use gaslighting to a large degree, however, malignant narcissists are likely to be far more secretive with their methods. Nonetheless, any type of gaslighting is dangerous to the individual and their overall wellbeing. We should also point out that you don't have to be a narcissist to use gas lighting; many people without narcissism use this manipulation tactic from time to time, and it's certainly one which exerts control and causes distress in one of the most underhanded ways possible.

Borderline Personality

What Is a Borderline Personality

Have an open and determine presence because the very that you've opened this book to read is one step towards wanting to change the way your mind perceives things, it is one step towards wanting to make sense of your thoughts and emotions, and it is also one step towards starting or working towards a life that is fulfilling and purposeful.

Do you know someone who is struggling with borderline personality disorder (BPD)?

Or maybe it is you who have it, and you're trying to figure out if it is BPD or something else entirely? No matter the case, up-to-date, accessible and accurate information on this disorder is a necessity. If you are looking for information that is not too technical and confusing, with accurate facts, then this compassionate book is for you.

What is Borderline Personality Disorder

BPD or borderline personality disorder is a serious psychological condition that makes it difficult for a person to feel comfortable in themselves. It is characterized by unstable moods and emotions, behavior as well as relationships which makes it hard for people to control their impulses and emotions. BPD is one of the several personality disorders recognized by the American Psychiatric Association (APA).

BPD commonly begins in adolescence or early adulthood, and it can continue for a long period of time, often causing serious issues when relating to the people around them. If left untreated, BPD can cause a great deal of distress. People with BPD have high levels of anger, often taking offense at things people say or do. They also have high levels of distress and struggle with beliefs, and painful thoughts about themselves, as well as the people, come to know. BPD has a serious impact on almost every aspect of the person's life, from family, relationships, siblings, social as well as work life. Some people with BPD also resort to harming themselves.

Symptoms usually begin during their teen years or as a young adult, some improve as they get older, but most don't without the right treatment. It is important for you to realize that

Why is it called 'Borderline'?

The word borderline is added to this order simply due to historical reasons. Before medical science and therapy science began to develop, BPD was categorized as a 'neuroses' and 'psychoses' by psychiatrists. When it was first being researched and written about, BPD did not fall into any of the above-mentioned categories, so psychiatrists decided to put it in its own category, on an imaginary line between 'psychoses' and 'neuroses.'

When is Borderline Personality Disorder Diagnosed?

Doctors or psychiatrists look for five major symptoms or criteria that you have experienced to evaluate and assess if you have BPD. Apart from these five factors, they also investigate the time period of these symptoms if they have lasted for a considerable amount of time:

- You worry about people abandoning you

- You have intense emotions that last anywhere between a few hours to a few days, and it can also change quickly

- You do not have a strong sense of who you are, and it also changes depending on who you are with

- You also find it difficult to make and keep stable relationships

- You act impulsively and do things that harm yourself

- You feel emptiness

- You often self-harm

- You also have suicidal feelings

- You have intense feelings of anger, and you find it difficult to control

- You may also experience dissociation as well as paranoia

Getting a diagnosis for a mental disorder can answer many of the questions running through your mind and bring you calmness as it can help formulate proper treatment and speed up you or your loved one's recovery process. The issue with BPD is that it is difficult to diagnose. Many of the symptoms associated with BPD, such as impulsivity and self-image, are common in other disorders as well. For children, it can also be difficult to diagnose BPD as their brain and mind are still in early development and is constantly changing.

A study found in Psychiatric Times reported that among the adolescents that showed symptoms of BPD between the ages of 15 to 18, only 40 percent of them met the specific criteria two years later. Research on BPD is still not substantial enough, which makes treatment even more difficult. However, if your child is under the age of 18 and you believe that they may have BPD with symptoms that have maintained over at least 1 year, then they may be diagnosed with this disorder.

I want to Control My Thoughts

According to Dr. Catherine Pittman, a clinical psychologist, and professor at Saint Mary's College Psychology department, people who have high levels of overthinking due to Borderline Personality Disorder are because of pathological reasons. She goes on to say that the average person does overthink and that overthinking is rooted in the feeling of uncertainty.

To scientists, there is no clear reason as to why the process of overthinking happens in a person with BPD. This overthinking symptom causes many other issues such as impulsivity, distress, creating unnecessary panic and fear, and causing the person to react in very dangerous ways in the hopes of quietening the mind.

However, researchers can agree on one thing they all agree that overthinking engages the same parts of the brain that triggers fear, as well as anxiety in a person with Borderline Personality Disorder. According to Pittman, the cerebral cortex in the human brain is the center of all thinking, and it is a logical part of the brain that is related to memories. It also helps us think about and anticipates things.

But the danger lies when you start obsessing about something, and it triggers the amygdala's attention. Amygdala's attention is the brain's emotional system, and through research, scientists have found it to include fear and, yes, anxiety. When we experience fear, anxiety, or panic, the amygdala is the reason that our heart pounds, our muscles tense up, and it makes us feel uneasy.

The more you worry about something, the more you train your brain to overthink and, eventually, the more you activate the amygdala. It is a vicious cycle, no doubt, and you end up putting yourself at risk of getting anxiety disorders.

Could my diagnosis be wrong?

What is I am not happy with the diagnosis given to me by my doctor? What do I do? The process of diagnosing BPD is a long one, and if you have a young child you feel may have BPD, it is advised to seek treatment right away to help out with the more obvious symptoms the child may have rather than to wait for a diagnosis. Diagnosis takes long simply because you want someone who listens, who is an expert in treating BPD and above all, non-judgmental. That said, many BPD signs may be very similar to types of mental disorders, which make diagnosing hard.

These symptoms include:

- bipolar disorder

- depression

- psychosis

- antisocial personality disorder (ASPD)

Depending on what is going in your life at the moment as well as your mood, it can affect what you tell your therapist or mental health care professional, and it makes it hard for them to pinpoint exactly what diagnosis best fits your signals and experiences. They may also provide treatment that is entirely different from that of BPD. Also, you or your child may experience other mental health issues and BPD at the same time.

What can I do if I disagree with my diagnosis?

If you're concerned that the diagnosis given to you doesn't suit what you are going through, you can get a second opinion from another expert in mental health or a therapist so that you can be sure that the right treatment is available to support you.

Do not be afraid of getting a second opinion it is always best to know what you have rather than to doubt and second guess, which might just aggravate your symptoms.

Different views on BPD diagnosis

A possibility of a broad diagnosis is high when it comes to BPD or EUPD simply because you only need to experience at least five of the challenges discussed above. This often also includes a lot of different people and different experiences. Many people find it beneficial to get a diagnosis because it gives them a sense of relief and credibility as well as answers. It also helps them to understand their difficulties and make sense and provide validation of what they are going through. But for some, a diagnosis is not helpful at all. They may disagree with the entire system of diagnosing personality disorders, find it unhelpful and even stigmatizing. Some people do not want to label their experiences as a medical issue or consider it a disorder.

If this is any help, take comfort in the fact that any diagnosis, any therapy session, any conversation you have with your doctor or therapist is entirely confidential. A diagnosis or at the very least, a discussion with your therapist will enable you to find an answer or to make sense of the symptoms you have. You would also receive the support you need as well as know that you are not alone in this.

Why is Early Diagnosis Crucial?

It is crucial to get a person who has developed symptoms into treatment as soon as possible, especially if BPD is taken as a lack of emotional regulation. The individual concerned needs to get into treatment before more maladaptive behavior sets in.

This is extremely crucial for young people who are during developing their sense of self and identity, which is made even more tough for young people with BPD symptoms. When the environment you are in does not reflect on what your experience feels like, it will get harder to know who you are and what your beliefs and values are too. Another crucial element to get an early diagnosis of BPD is to reduce any inaccurate diagnosis that shares similar symptoms such as depression, ADHD and bipolar disorder. These are sometimes co-occurring disorders, which could also be misdiagnosed. Because of these inaccuracies, teenagers who are given medications such as mood stabilizers and antipsychotics often find that they are ineffective.

Some adolescents are often on extensive drug cocktails because their therapists do not know what exactly is happening and often just go after treating the specific symptoms without any accurate validation.

What Causes a Borderline Personality Disorder

The exact causes of borderline personality disorder are not established, although this is an area that doctors continue to study. Experts in the field do agree that there are certain contributing factors, both environmental and biological, that increase a person's risk of developing a borderline personality disorder. These are:

1. Genetics: Studies have shown that over 60% of those diagnosed with borderline personality disorder suffer from genetic abnormalities that affect the brain's pathways responsible for the cognitive activity, impulse control, and the way the brain processes emotions. This is the reason why BPD is manifested by a lack of logical perception and reasoning.

While it is agreed that there isn't a single gene that is responsible for the development of borderline personality disorder, it is also hereditary as it can be passed down from one generation to another. First degree relatives, including parents, children, or siblings of those who have BPD, are 10 times more likely to be diagnosed with the same disorder some time in their lives. Borderline personality disorder studies that have focused on twins also confirmed that the illness is hereditary. People can inherit temperament and other personality traits which include aggression and impulsiveness.

2. Brain abnormalities: The brains of those who have borderline personality disorder share common characteristics:

The hippocampus, which makes up a significant part of the limbic system which regulates emotions, is smaller in those who have BPD. The same feature is also observed in those who suffer from post-traumatic stress disorder.

The amygdala may also be smaller and more active for those diagnosed with BPD. The amygdala is an almond-sized set of neurons in the brain, responsible for processing emotions both positive and negative. The unusually strong activity in the amygdala may be the reason why those with BPD exhibit more heightened negative emotions including shame, fear, anger, and sadness.

The prefrontal cortex, responsible for decision making, personality expression, complex cognitive behavior, and social behavior, is less active in those who have BPD. In particular, it is less active when the patient is observed as they are recalling feelings of fear and abandonment. Since the prefrontal cortex is responsible for stimulating emotions, the inactivity in this part of the brain could be the primary reason why those with BPD have difficulties controlling their emotions and managing stress.

The hypothalamic-pituitary-adrenal axis which is responsible for cortisol production, is more active in those who have a borderline personality disorder. Cortisol is released as the body's response to stress, and an increase of it in the body may result in a higher incidence of irritability which is observed in those who have BPD. If a person has experienced traumatic events in their past, this may also lead to increased cortisol production.

3. Environmental factors: A person's behavior is shaped by their experiences in life; particularly in relation to one's childhood as well as the relationships with parents or families as a whole. While various environmental factors may be responsible for borderline personality disorder, the most critical always seems to be poor parenting. A child who experiences separation from one or both parents, who experienced physical, verbal, or sexual abuse by a family member, or who received little to no care, are at high risk for developing a borderline personality disorder.

However, it is still important to note that children who do not experience abuse or traumas within their family can still develop a borderline personality disorder. In this scenario, biological causes are at play and are significant enough to cause BPD.

4. Estrogen: Varying estrogen levels in women may also be responsible for causing borderline personality disorder. The effects of estrogen on the brain chemistry of women's reproductive hormones are very complex. This is because estrogen levels can lead to a fluctuation of other hormones. Examples of these include:

A decrease in dopamine levels, the neurotransmitter responsible for reward, memory, and behavior;

Varying effects on serotonin levels, which is responsible for producing feelings of happiness and well-being;

Increased production of endorphins in the brain and the blood, which is responsible for feelings of euphoria and inhibiting the transmission of pain signals;

Increased norepinephrine levels, which contracts the heart as a response to stress

Studies have shown that BPD symptoms exhibited by women changed according to their menstrual cycle due to the estrogen levels in their bodies. This is a reason why women who suffer from pre-menstrual syndrome are often misdiagnosed for borderline personality disorder. They exhibit the same characteristics such as extreme mood swings, depression, sadness, and irritability.

5. Society and Culture: People who live in societies with higher incidences of unstable family relationships are more prone to developing a borderline personality disorder. The combination of poor lifestyle choices, impulsiveness, and other symptoms of BPD increases a person's chances of risky situations. For this reason, adults who live with BPD are more vulnerable to being victims of rape, violence, as well as other crimes.

6. Child Abuse: There are different kinds of child abuse and neglect that contribute to borderline personality disorder. Physical abuse occurs when a caregiver or parent hurts a child with the intention of injury. Disciplinary measures that entail a physical aspect is not considered to be child abuse if the child does not have an injury.

Sexual abuse is when a child is forced to engage in sexual behavior, not limited to fondling or assault. Other acts that constitute sexual abuse include occasions when an adult exposes their genitals to a child, takes photographs of a child as they are naked with the intent of using it for sexual purposes, or forces a child to engage in sex.

Emotional abuse can come in the form of withholding love, insults, threats, and constant criticism. Emotional abuse does not leave visible scars, unlike physical abuse. However, emotional abuse can harm a person psychologically for a long period of time.

Neglect is also a form of child abuse and occurs when a parent or caregiver is unable to meet a child's basic needs including shelter, food, education, safety, and emotional support. When a child is left alone without proper adult supervision this also constitutes neglect.

Symptoms of Borderline Personality Disorder

The primary signs that a person may be suffering from borderline personality disorder is an evident pattern of unstable personal relationships, negative self-image, and being too emotional. People with BPD are also usually very impulsive and may resort to self-destructive behavior such as suicide attempts and risky sexual behavior. Symptoms of BPD are consistent and observed in a wide range of social as well as personal situations. Eventually, if left untreated, these can lead to added stress and inability to function properly in social and work situations. The patterns are also noticeable because they are stable and tend to be long in duration.

1. Emotional Instability: BPD is also referred to as Emotionally Unstable Disorder because it is the prevalent characteristic in most cases. This is characterized as impulsivity, a rapid shift in emotions, chaotic relationships, and hostility. It is also common for people with BPD to jump from one emotional crisis to another.

While most people tend to experience impulsivity and rapid mood shifts during adolescence, those with borderline personality disorder exhibit it later in life although it will last for a longer period of time. Adults who have BPD tend to suffer from extreme mood swings and anger. It is also normal for people to experience occasional mood shifts and emotional changes but for those who have BPD, these episodes are much more intense that it will impact their work, social, and personal lives.

Those with borderline personality disorder also have other problems with emotions. They tend to feel more negative emotions than other people. They also feel more "empty" and in fact, may even describe the feeling as though they have nothing inside.

People with a borderline personality disorder also feel emotions more intensely than others. It is not uncommon to meet people with BPD who live generally joyful and happy lives, but when they encounter negative emotions they instantly feel overwhelmed. Examples of these are instead of feeling sadness, they feel grief; instead of feeling embarrassed they feel humiliation and shame; instead of being annoyed they experience rage; instead of feeling nervous they panic. For this reason, people with BPD are extremely sensitive to feelings associated with failure, isolation, and rejection.

Since they are not able to cope with these intense emotions they may result in self-harm. People with BPD are aware of the fact that they are having difficulties dealing with negative emotions and because they are unable to find an outlet to cope they try to shut off these emotions completely.

Mood swings are part of the emotional instability experienced by individuals who have a borderline personality disorder. These mood swings can happen often, in fact someone with BPD may go through many episodes in the course of a day. On the other hand, a mentally healthy person will experience mood swings just twice in a week. The mood swings brought about by borderline personality disorder are consistent over time.

There are also distinguishing features of mood swings caused by BPD. The primary difference is that BPD mood swings are caused by triggers, usually when the trigger is related to perceived rejection by another person. However, if a person is suffering from mood swings alone it is not enough to diagnose them of borderline personality disorder since it is just one of the many symptoms.

2. Impulsive behavior: Impulsive behavior is common in people with a borderline personality disorder. It refers to acting quickly on something without contemplating the consequences of one's actions. Acting on impulse is usually a response to an event that causes extreme emotions that are usually negative, but for those with a borderline personality disorder, they act impulsively as a way to deal with their emotions. It provides them with immediate relief from pain.

Common characteristics include alcohol or substance abuse, risky sexual behavior include participation in unprotected sex with multiple partners, reckless driving, irresponsible spending, and eating disorders. They also tend to change jobs and leave relationships more often. While it is normal for people to participate in these impulsive activities occasionally, for those with BPD it lasts for a longer period of time because they see these activities as an attempt to restore some normalcy in their lives and respond to extreme emotion. Impulsive behavior is one of the most troubling aspects of borderline personality disorder because it can lead to severe health problems, relationship issues, financial woes, and even legal issues down the line.

People with a borderline personality disorder also experience feelings of shame and guilt after giving into their impulsive behavior. It is a dangerous cycle that involves feeling extreme emotions, resorting to impulsive behavior as a way of relieving their pain, then immediately feeling shameful and guilty about their behavior, resulting in emotional pain. This all leads to more extreme emotional pain to which a person with BPD will resort to new impulsive behavior in order to cope with their new pain. Over time, impulsive behavior will become an automatic way of dealing with emotional pain. This cycle explains why many people with borderline personality disorder tend to become addicted to different things that give them temporary relief from their emotions. For the same reason, it is also why addiction and impulsivity in borderline personality disorder overlaps.

The common characteristics of people suffering from addiction and borderline personality disorder include:

- Impulsive and harmful behavior
- Severe mood swings ranging from depression and feelings of joy
- Manipulative actions
- A lack of concern for one's health and safety
- Pursuing dangerous activity despite the high risks involved
- A pattern of instability in finances, relationships, and jobs

The relationship between borderline personality disorder and addiction can be rather volatile. Drug and substance abuse will further aggravate the other dangerous symptoms of BPD particularly depression and anger. In some cases, this leads to more profound feelings of emotional emptiness.

Dialectical Behavior Therapy (DBT) is the best course of treatment in addressing this co-occurring disorder. It teaches skills such as mood awareness, meditation exercises, and training in social skills where the end goal is to reduce one's impulsivity. One of the key features of DBT that is useful in treating impulsivity is mindfulness which helps people become more aware of the consequences of the actions they are about to engage in. With the practice of mindfulness, impulsive people take the time to make better informed and healthy decisions as well as have better responses even in the light of extreme emotions and stress.

Some medications may also help reduce the symptoms of impulsivity in a person. However, the drugs are only effective when they are used together with psychotherapy. It should be noted that medication should not be the first course of treatment for impulsivity although it is useful for BPD and other co-occurring disorders. Antidepressants such as selective serotonin reuptake inhibitors are effective in treating impulsive behavior that occurs with a borderline personality disorder. Other medicines such as Effexor and Serzone have been shown to reduce symptoms of impulsivity.

3. Unstable Relationships: People suffering from BPD are not capable of having stable personal relationships. They cannot be alone for long periods of time because they also tend to suffer from abandonment anxiety. People with a borderline personality

disorder will try to hide their manipulative characteristics and dependency on their partners.

The inability to have lasting, stable relationships is also connected to impulsive behavior stemming from borderline personality behavior. Promiscuity and substance abuse create conflict with romantic partners, resulting in separation, divorce, and even domestic violence.

People who suffer from BPD have difficulty trusting other people. They feel irritable and angry, exhibiting temper tantrums even toward people that they care for. Because people with borderline personality disorder have a distorted view of what is socially acceptable, they experience difficulty in trusting people and cooperating with others. If they experience challenges within their relationships, they don't respond in a manner that would help to repair it, unlike others. Doing this severely limits their capacity to be fully cooperative in romantic relationships as well as friendships.

The main reason why people with borderline personality disorder find it difficult to focus on the emotions of other people is that they themselves are too overwhelmed with their own feelings. They find that their emotional pain is a major obstacle. Individuals with a borderline personality disorder also tend to feel that regardless of what their partner does, their emotional needs are never met. In spite of this, they don't have the ability to assert what they need in a healthy, productive manner. This results in frustrations because at the end of the day they don't get what they want and they feel angry.

People with BPD lack the skills to manage their anger and end up lashing out at their partners. Many cases of sexual and physical aggression towards partners are associated to borderline personality disorder.

Additionally, individuals with BPD view relationships as black or white. For them, people are either all good or all bad, there is no middle ground. In relationships, this kind of mentality devalues one's partners. But since they have extreme fears of abandonment, they may also resort to manipulation to prevent their partners from leaving them.

In particular, men who have borderline personality disorder can be emotionally explosive. Men with BPD are usually jealous, depressive, and angry most of the time. They may resort to physical aggression once they feel that their female partners are placing a distance between them, whether socially or emotionally.

This kind of behavior is also observed in lesbian relationships wherein one partner is suffering from a borderline personality disorder. These situations found one partner resorting to violence when they felt that their partner was becoming physically or emotionally distant in the relationship. Studies have also shown that women with BPD are at higher risk of using aggression in relationships than those without BPD.

Couples wherein one partner suffers from borderline personality disorder usually have to turn to counseling as a form of therapy. It is necessary for each person in the relationship to see a therapist separately from the other so that they can each work on their own issues followed by addressing the relationship as a whole. There are therapists specializing in borderline personality disorder who can help couples manage their relationships better and move forward despite BPD.

4. Identity disturbance: People with BPD don't have a stable secure personality or sense of self. They are more sensitive to their environment and the people that they spend time with. As a result, they will end up adopting habits, values, and even mimicking the attitudes of the people they spend time with the most.

Identity disturbance is also characterized by sudden but intense changes in a person's image. The instability in one's identity can also result in dramatic changes in career, values, life goals, types of friends, sexual identity, and even opinions.

5. Paranoia: In some cases, people with a borderline personality disorder also suffer from paranoia. They are overtly suspicious of other people's behaviors and intentions, sometimes feeling like everyone is out to get them. These episodes of paranoia may come and go, and are usually short-lived. At most, it can last for a few days and often occur in periods of distress or trauma. People with paranoia tend to think that the world is out to get them, and have fears that include people spying on them or that friends are talking behind their back.

Paranoid thinking can be mild and short-lived, although there are people that experience severe paranoia that lasts for months. Individuals that suffer from a delusional disorder or psychotic disorders have chronic, severe paranoia which is completely unrelated from anything going on in reality.

6. Fears of Abandonment: Unlike separation anxiety, people with BPD experience abandonment fears wherein they perceive separation or a change in routine in their near future. This will cause them to react by extreme changes in behavior, self-image, thought, and mannerisms. If the thought of abandonment traumatizes them, they may resort to self-harm and even attempt suicide as a means of coping.

Most people with BPD who suffer from abandonment issues don't realize it but their behavior tells it all. There are certain characteristics of people with BPD that are related to their fear of abandonment. These include:

Staying in an unhealthy relationship because they cannot overcome their fear of being alone. Oftentimes people with BPD have extreme fears of abandonment that even if they are in a dysfunctional relationship that does not benefit them in any way whatsoever, they refuse to get out of it as they have formed a dependency on their partner. As a result, both partners end up staying in a relationship that is full of conflict and drama.

Fear of abandonment may also be manifested through depression because the sadness is turned inwards.

People who have abandonment issues may show rage to people that they love. While it sounds like the complete opposite behavior you would expect from someone who does not want to be left by a loved one, people with BPD feel vulnerable and helpless and may end up lashing at their partner to regain a sense of control.

It is common for partners to experience being harassed by their partners who have BPD. It may be in the form of being bombarded by phone calls, texts, and emails because a person with BPD constantly needs reassurance that they will not be abandoned. Furthermore, fear of abandonment causes people to find solitude or isolation completely unbearable and constantly trying to be in contact with their partner.

The cause of abandonment issues in people with borderline personality disorder varies. For some, it may be traumatic childhood issues that stemmed from neglect or abuse by a caregiver. Children who have been adopted experienced the separation of their parents, or had a loved one die are also more prone to abandonment issues later on.

7. Anger: Most people with borderline personality disorder feel angry all the time. They may or may not express it, but the feelings of anger or rage are there. Their anger may be caused by a variety of factors but primarily it is a result of feeling neglected, ignored, or uncared for especially by people they are close to. People with BPD may also feel shameful or guilty if they express their anger.

8. Dissociation: Defined as a form of attachment that leaves a person feeling unreal and numb, dissociation usually occurs on its own. Everyone can experience dissociation at some point in their lives, where they feel like they just went on automatic pilot in a particular situation. Because borderline personality disorder is

considered a dissociative disorder, it gives the feeling that one is merely going through the motions of life without actually having any control. People who experience dissociation end up doing things without feeling emotions or connecting to the situation or people at all. In conditions of extreme dissociation, people can sometimes experience a complete block in memory. They are unable to recall situations where they encountered trauma, abuse, and major stress as a survival mechanism.

For some people, the intensity of BPD symptoms doesn't last and in fact, may decrease over time. This may be attributed to age, although there is no explanation yet on why some symptoms remain and others decline. There are some theories that attempt to explain this:

Treatment and knowledge of borderline personality disorder can greatly reduce the symptoms' intensity through the years. This is an obvious reason, as people who receive treatment and learn how to improve their lifestyles eventually reduce the problems they encountered before which was a result of BPD behavior.

Burn out may also occur as BPD symptoms lessen with age. It is also a fact that individuals with borderline personality disorder just engage in less impulsive activities.

People with BPD may also reduce interpersonal relationships altogether after many years of conflict and drama. Simply put, they avoid forming relationships to avoid problems.

Despite the observable decline of BPD symptoms in people as they age, there is no substitute for treatment. It is not a reason for people to avoid seeking help, thinking that things will improve in time. BPD people already put their lives at enough risk with impulsive behavior and miss out on living their lives to their full potential.

9. Self-harm: Self-harm is a common symptom in people with a borderline personality disorder. However, it is not to be confused with suicide because the two are completely different. Individuals resort to self-harm as a method of numbing emotional pain or as a way of punishing themselves. People also engage in self-harm as a way of reducing suicidal thoughts. In some cases, people with BPD fear that if they stop giving in to the urges to harm themselves they may actually become suicidal.

10. Suicide: Almost 80% of people with BPD have attempted suicide at least once in their lifetime. Unfortunately, around 10% of these people will actually succeed at their suicide attempts. This is why it is necessary for those with a higher suicidal risk to be treated with inpatient methods and be confined in hospitals where they will be detached from anything that they can use to harm themselves.

Therapies for Borderline Personality Disorders

Each person's experience with a borderline personality disorder is different. Some symptoms may be more dominant; while for one he could be more paranoid, for another he would be more dissociative. Depending on the situation and circumstances, a therapist can recommend the right treatment for borderline personality disorder.

In addition, it may be tempting for some people with BPD to attempt managing the disorder without resorting to therapy. In order to fully recover from the symptoms, one must be able to learn coping skills that they need to manage BPD every day. The urge to manage BPD without professional therapeutic help may have stemmed from negative experiences with doctors and therapists in the past. But without the commitment to recover fully from a borderline personality disorder, the chances of overcoming the symptoms are highly unlikely without the guidance of therapy.

Therapy teaches important life skills that are needed by people who suffer from BPD if they want to enjoy living a normal life again. These life skills are also crucial if the patient wants to enjoy a quality life. There are many resources on how one can self-help to reduce symptoms of BPD, but without the guidance of a licensed professional who is dedicated to helping you manage your disorder, you will never have an objective understanding or know if you have actually recovered from your illness.

The recovery process can be difficult alone, which is why this book discusses how family, friends, and loved ones can provide actual support. The moral support lent by loved ones will be valuable in recovery. Additionally, because borderline personality disorder is an actual mental condition, it is not advisable to go about it without professional intervention. If BPD is left untreated it can lead to serious consequences on oneself and to loved ones.

When one has BPD it can oftentimes be a scary experience that leaves one feeling isolated because it causes a strain on relationships. Individuals with BPD need the guidance of therapists to overcome this aspect of the disorder so that they can go back to their normal life and benefit from the joy that healthy human relationships can bring. Treatment for BPD can provide people with valuable skills that they need to carry out into the world for maintaining interpersonal relationships. Additionally, treatment can reduce the stress involved through the prescription of medication that decreases BPD symptoms.

Psychotherapy

Psychotherapy is the most common treatment of choice for people with mental illnesses especially those who have BPD. Although there are many forms of psychotherapy, they all have one goal in common and that is to help patients better understand the way their thoughts and emotions operate. It is an important aspect of treatment because while medication can help reduce certain symptoms of borderline personality disorder, it will not teach patients how to learn coping skills or regulate emotions the way psychotherapy does.

Psychotherapy is also crucial in helping people refrain from committing suicide. This is why therapists and other medical professionals involved stay in touch with the patient, constantly evaluating their vulnerability to suicide throughout the entire treatment. When a patient has severe feelings of suicide, hospitalization is the next step.

Dialectical Behavior Therapy

The most famous and effective form of psychotherapy known today is Dialectical Behavior Therapy or DBT. It was founded by Marsha Linehan and is a program that teaches people how to take better control of their lives and emotions. DBT also has a strong focus on emotion regulation, self-knowledge, and cognitive restructuring. DBT has a comprehensive approach and is usually conducted with a group. However, the skillset taught through Dialectical Behavior Therapy is considered complex and therefore not recommended to people who have difficulty learning new concepts.

Dialectical Behavior Therapy utilizes two concepts: validation and dialectics. In validation, the client is taught to accept that their emotions are real, acceptable, and valid. On the other hand, dialectics is a form of philosophy which teaches that life is not to be seen as black and white. It also reinforces the importance of accepting ideas even though they are contradicting one's own beliefs.

The primary goal of DBT is to help the client break their notions of the world and enjoy freedom from living a rigid life that causes one to resort to self-destructive behavior. DBT is held in weekly group as well as individual sessions. Clients are given a number that they can call any time if they feel that their symptoms are getting worse and need emergency assistance. In order for DBT to be effective, teamwork is expected. Clients need to work closely with their therapists as well as the other people met during group sessions.

While Dialectical Behavior Therapy is generally the most successful form of treating BPD, it has shown to be particularly useful in treating those who are more prone to suicide. Individuals with BPD resort to suicide because they feel that they have lost absolutely all control in life and suicide is the only thing they can do that can help them. Dialectical Behavior Therapy is particularly effective in helping people regain a sense of control in their lives. Once DBT has helped a patient be in control, therapists can focus on other aspects of their life to improve.

Therapists specializing in DBT work with those who are prone to suicide by engaging them in mindfulness, interpersonal effectiveness, emotion regulation, and distress tolerance. When people with BPD learn that there are healthy ways of coping and handling one's emotions, the risk of them committing self-harm and suicide are significantly decreased.

Borderline personality disorder, just like other personality disorders, is challenging to treat. Because the goal of treatment is to change the way a person views the world, stress, and other people, treatment is usually lengthy. Treatment for BPD is usually at least a year but can go on for much longer.

There are also other forms of psychotherapy that are used to address borderline personality disorder that focus on conflict resolution and social learning theory. These are more solution-focused therapies that fail to address the core issue of people who suffer from BPD which is difficulty regulating their emotions.

Schema Focused Therapy

Schema Focused Therapy is a type of psychotherapy whose primary goal is to identify and treat unhealthy ways of thinking. Some elements of schema-focused therapy include elements that are also found in cognitive behavioral therapy (CBT) and combines it with other methods of psychotherapy.

Schema focused therapy is founded on the principle that if a person's basic childhood needs such as love, acceptance, and a desire for safety are inadequate, this results in the development of unhealthy ways of thinking about the world. These are referred to as maladaptive early schemas. Schemes are defined as broad patterns of behavior and thinking. They are more than simply beliefs because they are closely held patterns that affect the way one perceives and interacts with the world.

The schema theory suggests that schemas occur when events in one's present life bear a resemblance to events in the past that are directly related to the creation of the schema. When a person has unhealthy schemas as a result of a difficult childhood, they will end up developing unhealthy ways of thinking as a response to the situation. Furthermore, schema theory suggests that the symptoms of borderline personality disorder are usually caused by a difficult childhood wherein a child may have experienced abandonment, trauma, or maltreatment by one or both parents, resulting in the development of maladaptive early schemas.

Schema focused therapy for borderline personality disorder seeks to identify relevant schemas in a person's life and tie them to schemas present in past events. A therapist works to help the patient process the emotional response that arises due to the schema. They then work on addressing unhealthy coping methods to help the patient respond to the scheme in a healthy manner. Schema focused therapy may involve exercises that are designed to halt unhealthy behavioral patterns, change the way one thinks, and encouraging the patient to vent out their anger.

Transference Focused Therapy

Transference Focused Therapy utilizes the patient-therapist relationship in order to improve how a person with borderline personality disorder sees the world. Transference is defined as the process wherein emotions are transferred from one person to the other. It is a key principle used in psychodynamic therapies where it is suggested that the way a client feels about persons that are important in their lives is transferred to his therapist. Through transference therapy, the therapist can clearly understand how the patient interacts with the people in his life in order to help them learn to effectively manage relationships. Eventually, the goal of transference focused therapy is to help patients enjoy having stable relationships again.

Therapists of transference focused therapy believe that symptoms of borderline personality disorder that arise from dysfunctional relationships one experienced during childhood continue in adulthood, thereby damaging the ability of these adults to have normal, healthy relationships. The interactions we have with our primary caregivers during childhood contributes to how we develop a sense of self and also affects how we perceive other people. If one does not have a healthy relationship with their caregivers during childhood, this results in adults having difficulty relating to other people and having a good sense of oneself.

Evidence shows that maltreatment or trauma or loss of caregivers during childhood increases one's risk of developing a borderline personality disorder. And because these symptoms have a negative impact, preventing one from developing relationships with people later on, some experts on BPD agree that it is important to address this by helping people focus on improving relationships through transference focused therapy.

With this kind of therapy, there is a focus on the relationship between the patient and the therapist. Unlike other forms of therapy where the therapist provides instructions on what the patient should do, transference focused therapy involves asking the client numerous questions during the discussion while they explore reactions. Furthermore, there is added emphasis on events that happen in the present moment instead of seeking out past experiences. For example, instead of spending time discussing issues with caregivers during one's childhood, the discussion is focused on how the client relates to their own therapist.

Therapists who practice transference based therapy are also skilled at remaining neutral, which is a reason why this kind of treatment is effective. They know not to give their opinion on their patient's reaction, and will also not be available outside session hours except for emergencies.

Mentalization-Based Therapy

Mentalization-based therapy (MBT) is another form of psychotherapy. MBT is based on the premise that people who have borderline personality disorder have difficulty thinking about their own thoughts. This means that people with BPD are unable to examine their own thoughts, beliefs, opinions and if they are realistic and useful to them. An example of this is when individuals with BPD may have sudden urges to harm themselves and end up giving in without thinking about the consequences of their actions.

MBT is also important because it helps people realize that others have their own thoughts and beliefs, and your own interpretation of their mental states is not always correct. Additionally, it helps people realize that actions will have an impact on other people's mentality. The main goal of MBT is to help clients recognize their own as well as others' mental states. It also teaches people with BPD how to step back from their own thoughts and examine if they are valid first. MBT may be conducted within a hospital as a form of inpatient therapy. Treatment is composed of daily sessions with a therapist as well as group sessions.

MBT usually lasts around 18 months, but depending on the need some patients may be asked to be an inpatient for the entire duration of their treatment. Some hospitals and treatment facilities will allow patients to leave at specified times during the course of their treatment.

Therapeutic Communities

Therapeutic Communities (TC) is a form of psychotherapy wherein people with various psychological conditions interact in a structured environment. This kind of treatment is best suited for those who have issues dealing with emotions and who are suicidal. By teaching them the skills needed for healthy social interaction with a wide range of people, people with a borderline personality disorder can better cope with their problems. TC therapy is usually residential and held in houses where clients stay 1-4 days a week.

Apart from individual and group sessions involved in TC, it also requires patients to participate in other activities designed to improve one's social skills and boost confidence. These activities include doing household chores, prepare and cook meals, play games, and participate in recreational activities. Therapeutic communities also involve all participants in regular community meetings where people with different psychological conditions meet in order to discuss issues and concerns within the community.

One of the unique features of the therapeutic community method of treatment is that it is run democratically. All members, including staff, can contribute their opinion on how TC's should be run. In fact, they can even vote if they think an individual should or shouldn't be admitted within the community. This means that even if one's therapist thinks that a therapeutic community is the best form of treatment for a case of borderline personality disorder, it doesn't mean that they will automatically be granted entry. Guidelines for acceptable behavior are defined in each TC because they set restrictions such as the prohibition of alcohol consumption, violence towards oneself and other members of the community. Members who break the guidelines may be asked to leave the TC.

Although a therapeutic community is one of the widely accepted methods of treatment for people with a borderline personality disorder, there is insufficient evidence to tell if a TC is effective for everyone. This is particularly the case for people with BPD who have difficulty following rules since TC's can be quite strict with guidelines.

Self-Care

Over the course of treatment, patients are usually given a telephone number that they can call if they think they are undergoing a severe crisis. It could occur when people with BPD are experiencing episodes of extreme symptoms and are more prone to self-harm and suicide. A number may be directed to the community mental health care practitioners, social workers, or other medical professionals. Depending on the area, a crisis resolution team service may also be available since they specialize in caring for people with serious mental health issues. Oftentimes these teams come to the rescue of individuals who may require hospitalization because of suicide attempts.

Those who suffer from borderline personality disorder usually find that merely talking to someone about what they are going through can help them get out of their crisis. Certain cases, although rare, may require medication such as tranquilizers to calm one's mood. Medications such as these are usually prescribed for 7 days to stabilize emotions.

Individuals with borderline personality disorder are encouraged to attend support groups for social support from those who are going through the same experience as they are. Support groups are useful in providing moral support through sharing common thoughts and feelings. Patients can also try coping skills and learn how to regulate their emotions with friends they make at these support groups. They have proven to be a crucial part of helping people with BPD expand their skill set while developing healthy social relationships and eventually reduce their symptoms in the long run.

If you are the one suffering from a borderline personality disorder, you may also find it challenging to take better care of yourself. However, those who are diagnosed with BPD should make it a priority to take better care of themselves because the symptoms may be exacerbated when one neglects self-care.

The basics of self-care involve engaging in activities that promote relaxation and good health. This means getting enough exercise, good sleep, taking the medications as prescribed by your therapist, eating nutritious food, and dealing with stress in healthy ways. People who take good care of themselves are less prone to suffering from psychiatric illnesses which are why self-care is necessary for everyone. It is especially important in those who are suffering from BPD because while it can not only worsen the symptoms, it can also result in slower recovery.

Many people tend to underestimate the importance of good sleep when it comes to proper self-care. If a person with BPD does not get adequate sleep they can become more anxious, irate, and aggressive. Here are some tips to help you get better sleep:

1. Avoid alcohol, nicotine, and caffeine a few hours before your bedtime. However, you will be able to sleep better if you completely eradicate these factors from your lifestyle.

2. Do not eat large meals before bedtime because it could cause upset stomach. Try to eat a light, filling meal at least three hours before you intend to go to sleep. On the other hand, don't go to bed with an empty stomach because a growling stomach caused by hunger can wake you up in the middle of the night and interfere with your sleep patterns. A warm glass of milk or a light snack are healthier alternatives.

3. Create a pre-bedtime ritual that will help you relax and soothe your mind. Some of these may include reading, aromatherapy, or taking a warm bath.

4. Establish a regular sleeping schedule which means avoiding naps, waking up at the same time each day, and sleeping at the same time every night.

5. Ensure that your bedroom is conducive to proper sleep. Lights should be turned off and noises reduced as much as possible. The temperature should also be just right.

People with borderline personality disorder should also pay close attention to diet and nutrition. Symptoms and moods can easily be affected by overeating, skipping meals, and eating food that has no nutritional value. Take supplements if needed, avoid fatty food, and make sure that you get a lot of fruits and vegetables each day.

Exercise also has an impact on mental health, this is why more doctors recommend their patients to live an active lifestyle. In addition, regular workouts increase the release of endorphins in the body, which help you feel more elated. Exercise works for the person with BPD by providing a healthy outlet for stress and stabilizing one's mood. Setting fitness goals for yourself and achieving them will also boost self-esteem and confidence.

People who already suffer from BPD are less likely to take good care of their health and suffer from other disorders that arise from a sedentary and unhealthy lifestyle later on. These include arthritis, obesity, high blood pressure, chronic fatigue syndrome, back pain, and urinary incontinence. Those who suffer from BPD are known to have unhealthy lifestyles: smoking cigarettes, consumption of alcohol, lack of exercise and proper sleep, and a dependency on pain medication. The symptoms of borderline personality disorder cause people to make poorer lifestyle choices because of stressful events or genetics, which will cause serious health problems down the line. Furthermore, the link between one's physical health and borderline personality disorder can be complex although more research is being conducted on it.

Given these facts, there are still many things you can do to improve the state of your health. Pay close attention to unhealthy habits that you can change today, such as quitting smoking and reducing your alcohol intake. Studies have shown that people who were once diagnosed with BPD and who recovered successfully no longer report health issues. Getting treatment for BPD can significantly reduce your chances of developing physical ailments and creating good habits.

Medications are another important aspect of self-care for people with BPD. While many people think that medication does not constitute self-care, those who are not committed to taking their medications regularly or take the incorrect doses may only exacerbate their symptoms and slow down recovery time. Avoid making changes to your medication without consulting your physician. On a similar note, not taking your medication at all is unhealthy and can have dangerous side effects.

Managing stress properly is also part of self-care. The presence of stress may be inevitable in our daily lives, and it does not mean that it is automatically a negative element. The key here is to learn how to manage stress effectively. Sometimes, stress may feel overwhelming and during these times you may need additional help to overcome them.

Medication

Some doctors agree that medication is useful in the treatment of people with a borderline personality disorder but others disagree. Today, there is still no medication that is licensed for the treatment of BPD. However, some forms of medicine have proven useful in reducing symptoms in certain people.

Usually, selective serotonin reuptake inhibitors (SSRI) are by default the first kind of medication that is prescribed to patients. SSRI's are designed to reduce impulsivity, depression, anger, suicidal behavior, and anxiety in people who suffer from mental health problems.

Medications such as anti-depressants and anti-anxiety pills may be useful to reduce symptoms, especially during a crisis or emergency. The most common kinds of antidepressants prescribed for patients of borderline personality disorder include Prozac, Zoloft, Nardil, Wellbutrin, and Effexor. However, this kind of medication is not encouraged for long-term use particularly because depression and anxiety are often short-term symptoms that may come and go as a result of various stressors in a person's life.

Antipsychotics also have a positive effect on patients even though they don't suffer from BPD. These are effective in reducing paranoia, anxiety, hostility, anger, as well as impulsivity in people with a borderline personality disorder. Common antipsychotic medications include Haldol, Clozaril, Risperdal, Seroquel, and Zyprexa.

Mood stabilizers are another form of medication that is used to treat symptoms of borderline personality disorder. These are effective in treating impulsivity, mood swings, and the intense changes in emotions caused by BPD. Common types of mood stabilizers include Lithobid, Depakote, Tegretol, and Lamictal.

Medications that specializes in reducing anxiety are known as anxiolytics, and are also prescribed for BPD. While anxiolytics are given to patients of borderline personality disorder, there is still insufficient evidence on the effectiveness of these medications in treating BPD as a whole. In fact, there have been cases where certain types of anxiolytics, known as benzodiazepines, were shown to increase the symptoms of BPD in other people. Common types of anxiolytics used for BPD patients include Valium, Xanax, Ativan, Klonopin, and Buspar.

Studies are currently being done to test the effectiveness of other types of medication for borderline personality disorder. Findings from some studies have shown that taking supplements such as omega 3 fatty acids can reduce feelings of hostility and aggression in those suffering from BPD.

People with a borderline personality disorder also need to be consistent in taking the medication as prescribed by their doctor. Honesty is also crucial in the success of medication for treating BPD. If you are taking care of someone, you may encourage this by reminding them to be open about their medication, what they feel, if they missed taking it, and other concerns they might have about it.

Before accepting medications from a physician, it is necessary to discuss any side effects thoroughly. If the side effects seem harmful, other forms of medicine may be considered especially if it is clear that the side effects are greater than the benefits. Medication used for a borderline personality disorder may vary depending on the kind of medicine. Some of the common side effects are detailed below:

Antidepressants:

- Headache
- Insomnia
- Reduced appetite
- Sedation
- Sexual dysfunction
- Weight gain

Mood stabilizers:

- Acne
- Tremors
- Weight gain
- Gastrointestinal distress
- Antipsychotics:
- Akathisia
- Dry mouth
- Weight gain
- Sexual dysfunction
- Sedation

Anti-anxiety:

- Fatigue
- Sleepiness
- Mental slowness
- Memory problems
- Impaired coordination

How To Know If A Medication Is Working

When you start to take medication for borderline personality disorder, this will result in both emotional and physical changes. If a medication is working well, the first thing that you may notice is a positive change in the way you respond to situations. Although the change is usually gradual and subtle, people experience the benefits of medications in a different time frame from other people. In fact, positive changes are usually not felt unless they have been happening for some time. It is also common for other people to notice the changes in your emotional response before you do, so you may want to ask people that you are usually with if they notice any changes.

These are other indications to help you recognize when a medication is effective for you:

1. You no longer think about certain events or issues with the same frequency as before. Your pattern of thoughts is no longer inconsistent and no longer wanders from one subject to another. Although you may experience some fatigue when you begin treatment, there is a noticeable improvement in clarity and focus. It will also be easier to focus on one thought for a longer period of time.

2. Things, places, events, or people that used to trigger no longer have the same effect on you. There will also be sudden improvements in communicating better with other people.

3. When you face situations that used to give you anxiety, you now face it with a sense of calmness. However, if you are taking

benzodiazepines it is recommended to talk to your physician about this change in response.

4. Things that used to upset or anger you no longer elicits the same response.

Gender-Specific Treatment

Borderline personality disorder treatments focused on women are available to help them cope better because the way men and women manage their emotions when dealing with the illness will differ. This is why some patients prefer gender-specific treatment options. However, not all centers will have women-only treatment options available.

Each person's BPD case is as unique as their thumbprint. The important aspect of treatment is to find qualified professionals who can design a program that will be most effective for your individual needs and who may adapt as you start to recover from the illness.

Women who have borderline personality disorder are also at higher risk for developing co-occurring disorders such as eating disorders, anxiety, suicide, and depression. If you are experiencing these, it is necessary to find treatments that will also address co-occurring disorders.

Gaslighting

What Is Gaslighting?

Gaslighting is a form of mental abuse, and it is commonly used by narcissists. The term itself was pegged in 1938 because of a play. The play portrays a man attempting to make his wife insane by messing with the lights inside of their home. The wife in this play tries to point it out to her husband, and he completely denies that the lighting within the household is changing at all. She starts to question herself, and he gains control. He is gaslighting her, and this is a brilliant example.

Many people deal with narcissists on a daily basis; however, it is surprising how many don't understand what gaslighting is. Gaslighting is one of the narcissist's favorite tactics to get complete control and power within their relationship. It abuses their partner and makes them second guess every thought and idea that crosses their minds.

Sometimes you are dealing with a narcissist, and you have no choice about it.

For instance, if they are a parent or family member, it is likely you can't rid yourself of the burden that is them. Narcissism can also be experienced in romantic relationships, as well as one's of a friendlier nature. Realistically, any relationship in your life could involve a narcissist, and each one is going to be a challenge to deal with. In fact, it is not only hard to deal with. It is oftentimes hard to recognize.

Narcissists have huge egos, and they only know how to love themselves. They will go to great lengths to have people perceive them in a certain way. They often tell stories of grandeur and think that there is no one better than them. Most narcissists are charismatic and can draw the attention of a crowd very easily. This can make it easy to fall for them and for them to gain control of you and your life. Recognizing a narcissist early on is the best defense against them.

If your partner ever repeatedly tells you that you are making things up or that you are remembering something incorrectly, it is likely that they are trying to gaslight you. This happens slowly over the relationship until the victim can't understand reality as it actually is. If you are being affected by gaslighting, it is common to find yourself questioning reality, your relationship, or possibly your own level of sanity. These are all signs of gaslighting.

This tactic is not only a form of mental abuse, but it is also a form of emotional abuse. When a person suffers from emotional abuse, it will take a toll on every aspect of their life. It is likely that they will have very low self-esteem. It is also common for those who suffer from emotional abuse to have problems with anxiety and depression. They often feel a sense of helplessness. In a gaslighting situation, they will become dependent on their narcissistic partner in every way. They start to accept the abuse as something that is normal and acceptable.

As noted, emotional abuse causes a lot of damage throughout their entire life. It is likely that they will question or not understand their own feelings. Additionally, it is likely that they will not trust their instincts, and they may even question their sanity. When these types of behaviors become an everyday occurrence, it puts all of the power and control into the hands of the narcissist. Once someone is no longer able to trust their own thoughts and ideas, it is much more likely that they will stay in an abusive relationship regardless of how terrible it is for them and their well-being.

The victim of gaslighting will, obviously, suffer, but so will the people that care about them.

Victims of this type of manipulation withdraw from the people they love, and that love them. They no longer trust what their most trusted assets have to say or what they think. Oftentimes, their relationships with anyone other than the narcissist will dissolve completely. This is painful and has a negative impact on everyone that cares about the victim. Trying to make the victim understand that what is happening is not right is almost impossible. This is especially true in terms of narcissistic relationships that have been going on for some time.

In addition, gaslighting is exceptionally effective in keeping a person under the narcissist's thumb. Mental and emotional abuse are ways for the narcissist to gain power within the relationship. They will gain control by any means necessary, even at the expense of their partner's happiness and well-being. Gaslighting is only one of the many forms of manipulation that the narcissist will use to maintain the life that they find suitable.

The effects of gaslighting do not happen overnight. It takes quite a bit of time and is typically quite gradual. In the beginning, their tactic may just look like simple misunderstandings. However, over the course of time, the abusive behavior will become continuous.

People on the outside of the relationship may be able to see the pattern of it, but it is unlikely that the partner being affected by it will be able to see this perception.

There are several reasons that the abused party will not be able to understand it when their friends, families, or loved ones try to tell them what is actually happening. Most narcissists will do their best to isolate their partner, which can lead to breakdowns of important relationships in the inability to hear what the people that truly care about them have to say. Victims of this type of use can also become extremely anxious or confused. This can make talking to them extremely difficult.

Depression is another element that comes along with gaslighting. People tend to disassociate with what is actually going on around them. Additionally, they may experience a lack of trust with people that care about them the most.

One of the saddest things about being in a relationship with a narcissist that uses gaslighting tactics is that eventually, the partner that is being abused will feel as if they absolutely need the narcissist to survive. Due to the fact that they cannot define true reality, they feel that they need their narcissistic partner to define it for them.

This makes the situation insanely difficult to get out of. It takes a lot of time and effort to help somebody open their eyes and realize that the person they love the most is actually abusing them and taking advantage of them.

Gaslighting not only manipulates people, it, realistically, is also a form of brainwashing. It lays seeds of doubt in the victim in every area. They won't be able to perceive the world as an individual, they may lose their identity completely, and it is likely that they feel very little self-worth. The thoughts, statements, and accusations of the gaslighter are consistently falsifications that are deliberate.

Their intention is thought out to make the person they are dealing with feel crazy, and thus, the narcissistic gaslighter holds all of the power and control within the confines of the relationship.

It does not matter how intelligent you are when it comes to gaslighting. If you do not see the signs and take action quickly, it is very likely that you will succumb to the wishes of the narcissist in your life. This is due to the fact that it can be hard to recognize. There are misunderstandings in every relationship due to poor communication or simple human errors of memory, so it can be easy to brush off the signs of gaslighting, especially in the beginning.

There are a variety of different signs that you are dealing with a narcissist that is using gaslighting tactics.

We will go over these signs in more detail later on in this book. For now, simply know that if you notice constant miscommunications where you are the one in the wrong, it is possible that you are dealing with someone that actually means you mental and emotional harm. You must remember that this form of manipulation is a slow process. When you are aware of the experiences you face, by being present in the moment, it can offer you the protection you need to not proceed in a relationship with someone who utilizes gaslighting.

The narcissist loves the tactic of gaslighting because it is so hard to perceive. Tools like accusations, denial, lying, and misdirection are all used to throw the person they are focused on off the trail of truth. It often leaves them feeling as if the issues they bring forth are simply part of their imagination. Additionally, they end up feeling like everything is their fault because of the things that the narcissist says and does. Gaslighting truly can make a person feel insane.

How Narcissists Control You

Manipulation is not a good thing, no matter what form it takes. Mental manipulation is some of the worst out there. Oftentimes, mental manipulation is referred to as psychological manipulation. Many people have experienced mental manipulation in their life; however, not everyone recognizes it. If you have not recognized it, it is likely that there have been very negative impacts on you because of it. Even if you do recognize it, depending on how long it has gone on for, the effects can be devastating.

Mental manipulation has the aim of changing the view of other people through deceptive or underhanded practices.

The manipulator will find advancement through these tactics, and more often than not, it is at the expense of another person.

This type of manipulation tends to emotionally exploit people so that the narcissist can gain power. Mental or psychological manipulation can be seen all over the world. From families to the workplace, it is unfortunate how often manipulation of this nature can be spotted.

It is important to understand that there is a difference between social influences that are healthy in nature and psychological manipulation. Most of us are influenced by people that we are in contact with. It is the compromise that we make in many of our relationships. These compromises are not manipulative but well thought out and understood in reality by both parties involved. Mental manipulation is quite different. It will solely benefit the manipulator regardless of the negative impact it causes for the other party. The imbalance of power is intentional. The manipulator's agenda is made possible by exploiting their victims.

There are a variety of different tricks that are commonly used by the person trying to mentally manipulate someone else. Knowing their tricks can better prepare you for how to deal with someone who is trying to exploit you for their own gain.

We are going to look over a variety of different tactics that mental manipulators may use to try and control you or get their own way.

The first thing a manipulator may do to try and gain power over you requires you to meet with them in a space that is theirs. Interaction in spaces that are considered to be theirs gives them more dominance. This could be their car, home, or even their office. These are spaces where they are dominant and have some sort of control. The feeling of ownership over the space gives them power, and they know that you will not feel a sense of ownership or familiarity, which makes it easier for them to stay in control during any discussions that are taking place.

The second thing a mental manipulator may do is always allow you to talk first. This may seem endearing in the beginning; however, it is absolutely a tactic that allows them to take control. They will let you speak so they can search for weaknesses and so they can understand your base pattern of thought. Salespeople use this trick frequently when they are trying to figure out if you will bite on what they have to offer. They will, in general, ask a lot of generic and probing type questions. These questions help them to figure out your thinking pattern and your behaviors. From there, they can figure out what your strengths and weaknesses are, allowing them to make an offer you simply can't refuse. This tactic of asking questions to attain a certain outcome can be done in personal relationships and within your workplace. You can really see it pretty much everywhere.

The next thing that the mental manipulator may do to take control of you or a situation is to falsify facts. They may lie or make excuses to throw you off guard. Mental manipulators tend to be very two-faced. They frequently like to make the victim believe that they are causing the problems themselves. They do this by altering the truth. It is also very likely that if you're dealing with a mental manipulator, they will withhold or change key pieces of information by exaggerating them or understating them.

The 4th sign of mental manipulation is overwhelming people with statistics or with facts. Narcissists tend to present themselves as experts in a variety of different areas. They try and take advantage of people by presenting them with statistics and empirical data to back up what they're saying. Typically, they will talk about topics that the person they're speaking with knows little about so that rebuttals cannot occur.

We see this 4th sign happen in a variety of different areas. It is common in financial situations, sales, negotiations, and even discussions between professionals. Additionally, it can be seen in social or relationship arguments.

Due to the fact that this tactic makes the person look like an expert, it gives them a sense of power over you.

It makes it easier for the manipulator to convince you to agree with their agenda. Sometimes there is no end game; it is simply to allow the manipulator to feel intellectually superior.

Next, mental manipulation can come in the form of extreme bureaucracy. Mental manipulators will try and use procedures, paperwork, laws, and committees to attain or keep their powerful position. This makes your life much more difficult, and the technique can be used to keep you from looking for the truth. It helps the manipulator to hide their weaknesses, flaws, and downfalls. It also allows them to evade judgments from other people.

Many mental manipulators will also use the tone of their voice and the emotion behind it to try and gain control. They believe that raising their voices will make people submit to them. This is a pretty aggressive form of manipulation, but it is surprising how often it works. An aggressive voice, paired with strong body language, certainly makes an impact. Many people will submit because these types of expressions are intimidating, and it is simpler to just lie down and follow what they are saying.

Negativity is frequently utilized by manipulators. They even go as far as to surprise people with negativity.

This allows them to throw you off balance and gain an advantage psychologically. This can be done in a variety of ways. A good example is someone letting you know at the last minute that they will not be able to hold up their end of a deal. The fact that they do it last minute is a clue, this coming at you with no warning does not give you time to prepare a counterattack. You may even find yourself making concessions so that the manipulator will keep working on the task they have agreed to do.

A lack of warning gives a person very little time to make an informed decision. This is a common tactic of salesmen, negotiators, and manipulators. When you put pressure on someone to make a decision by stating that something is a limited time offer or that there are consequences in not answering right now, it gives power to the person doing the persuading. Their demands are more likely to be met because of the tension that is caused by a lack of time.

Manipulators also like to hide behind sarcasm and humor. They will make remarks that are critical and try to pass them off as a joke. They understand that these types of digs will make you feel inferior, and your sense of security in yourself will be weakened.

They may make sarcastic comments on a variety of different things, including your looks, the age of your electronics, your credentials, or even your background. By trying to make you feel bad or look bad to your peers, they believe they will find superiority.

Alongside sarcasm and humor, manipulators are infamous for judging and criticizing others so that they feel inadequate. It is not as low key as negative humor. We say this because when a manipulator decides to go this route, they will ridicule, marginalized, or dismiss you openly. They do this to maintain superiority and keep you feeling off-balance. If they can grow the impression that you have something wrong regardless of how hard you are trying, you will likely start to feel inadequate or as if you could never be good enough in any way. When the negative is consistently focused on without any solutions, it is very damaging to a person's self-worth.

Another tactic that mental manipulators like to use is giving people the silent treatment. When you are trying to get ahold of somebody via a phone call, email, text message, or a variety of other ways and they deliberately don't respond, they gained power. This is due to the fact that they know that you are waiting on a response that they refuse to provide.

The intention is to place uncertainty in you.

They use silence as leverage, and it really is a head game that they are playing with you.

Mental manipulators are also fantastic at playing dumb. Feigning ignorance is one of their favorite tricks. They pretend that they have no idea what it is that you want or what it is that you are asking. When they do, this many people will take over the task themselves. We see children do this frequently so that they can talk their parents into doing the chore or task for them as they don't really want to do it. When adults use it, it is typically because they are trying to hide something or avoid an obligation.

The second to last tactic that emotional manipulators like to use is commonly referred to as guilt baiting. This is when a person targets another person's emotional weaknesses or vulnerabilities. It allows the manipulator to coerce someone into meeting their requests or demands. They frequently do this by blaming others. Additionally, if they know your soft spots, they will likely utilize them. You may even find that they make you feel responsible for their own happiness or their unhappiness.

The last trick that mental manipulators like to use is victimizing themselves. They will exaggerate their personal issues to get sympathy.

When the manipulator plays the role of the victim, it exploits the good nature of the person they are manipulating. Many people feel obligated to help others that are in need, and the manipulator knows this. They can reap the benefits of getting their own way by making you feel bad for them. You may even end up making concessions you would not normally make just to try and help them heal without ever realizing they are simply pulling one over on you.

How to Avoid Mental Manipulation

Now that we have looked at a variety of different tactics that the mental manipulator will try and use against you, we want to give you some tools to help you avoid it. Obviously, no one wants to be manipulated, and figuring out how to see what is happening and what to do about it can help ensure that you do not become a victim. There are so many different types of manipulation, and mental manipulation can be harder to see than others. Hopefully, you will be able to learn enough from this book to ensure your safety from these nefarious intentions.

One of the tricks that are favored by the mental manipulator is denying things that they have said.

You can easily combat this behavior by simply taking notes. Whether you do this in a notebook or on your phone, it provides you with hard evidence if the subject comes back up. Certain phrases stand out when you are having a discussion with the manipulator, and jotting them down puts some of the power back in your hands. This simple thing is very intimidating to the person trying to manipulate you, and it is likely they are going to become very defensive.

You do need to be a bit careful if you are going to use this tactic. You can try and tell your manipulator that you are writing things down because you are feeling forgetful, but that may not work. They are pretty skilled at recognizing things and then flipping them around on you. You may find that at the end of it, you are still the one that is feeling bad or guilty. If you are in a situation that you feel you need to write things down so they don't get twisted later, maybe you should ask yourself why this person is in your life at all.

Another thing you can do to help ensure that a mental manipulator does not gain power over you is to be mindful of what you are feeling. Mindfulness is simply being aware of what is truly going on inside of you. When manipulation occurs, it often leaves us feeling uncomfortable or uneasy.

You may feel defensive, guilty, angry, or even ashamed; these feelings are a good sign that the person you are dealing with may be manipulating you. Additionally, you may know you aren't doing anything wrong, but yet you feel as if you are. Here again, this is a good sign of psychological manipulation. When you are aware enough to recognize these signals, it can help you avoid falling into the trap being set by the manipulator.

Simply listening is another great tactic when you are dealing with a mental manipulator. They will consistently try and get you to agree with their point of view. When you listen, you may be able to understand their perspective, but it does not require you to agree with it. Sitting back and allowing the manipulator to talk will also provide you with the opportunity to think about what they're saying and balance yourself internally.

Manipulators oftentimes have an inane need to be heard, so listening gives them something they want, and it also keeps you protected as you will not necessarily have to change your perspective. It can also provide you with information about what motivates the person you are dealing with. This can help you find resolution in not only your current situation but in future ones as well.

Your experience and your values play a big role in your particular perspective. You can help yourself to avoid being manipulated by being firm in these areas. You need to have an understanding that your perspective is valuable, and it is also valid. When you maintain firm control over your perspective and position, it allows you to avoid caving in. This is true even when you are dealing with a manipulator holding the opposite perspective. By keeping ahold of your own perspective instead of caving in, you will be able to hold on to your own truths. This can help you not feel as confused by what the manipulator is saying. Take the time to learn your views and don't be afraid to ask for time to think things over. This will allow you to dictate what your true beliefs are on the situation instead of getting flustered and simply agreeing.

While some manipulation is derived from ill-intent, not all of it is. Oftentimes, manipulation is someone simply trying to get you to change your point of view, so it matches theirs. You should always let the person you are talking to know that you get where they are coming from. This is easiest to do by paraphrasing what they said and stating that you believe their intentions are good.

Many people don't even realize it when they are manipulating others.

We all tend to rationalize our behaviors. So, if they think you do not understand them or they feel that you think their intent is negative, it could lead to defensive words and actions. This could cause arguments that are easily avoidable by simply reflecting on what they said and validating them in their beliefs.

Stating and maintaining your position on any given subject can also help you avoid manipulation. Even if your counterpart can not accept your point of view, you should stay grounded in it unless you really do agree with what they have to say. If you don't, however, you should be willing to agree to disagree. This may not go over well with the manipulator, but they will have to accept it if you stay strong in your position on the topic.

By doing the above things, you are empowering yourself to avoid manipulation. These are only a few of the many tactics that can be enacted to ensure you safely avoid being manipulated. Know that sometimes trying to stay friends or in a relationship with a manipulator is impossible regardless of what you try. Some people are not going to allow any of these things to work, and then it is best to remove yourself from the toxic situation that manipulators can cause.

Effects of Gaslighting

Remember that you can get away from the abuse, but there are things that can happen if you're not careful, if you continue to stay in the presence of someone who gaslights you, and who abuses you.

What can happen though/ let's talk about what can happen if you continue to suffer at the hands of a gaslighter?

Memory Loss

This is what's so scary about gaslighting. When you experience gaslighting after a while, sometimes you'll start to feel so guilty and have a lot of self-doubts that you'll tend to forget things that happened. You may not know why it happened, and not remember things that happened between those time periods. Some people will even experience the abuser accusing them of something that happened, but they're unable to actually remember what happened.

Sometimes, what's scary about gaslighting is when you experience that, over a long period of time, you'll begin to realize that you can't remember the exact situations, because your mind and reality is completely skewered. You'll start to realize that you can't remember things that the abuser would accuse you of.

Sometimes, the abuser would accuse you of things that you're doing, but you don't remember doing them, and this, in turn, will lead you to wonder whether or not you did something. You'll definitely start to realize this as well when you get away.

Sometimes, they'll claim you're abusive, and how you hurt them, but you literally can't remember why. You oftentimes will try very hard to remember the abuse and trauma, but you can't.

Another type of way you can lose your memory with this is blanking on various things. When you're gaslit, you start to feel your reality starts to change, and you start to become an effect of the abuser that's there. However, sometimes after gaslighting happens, you can't remember all of the trauma you went through.

Perhaps it's a defensive mechanism, or maybe it's just your brain trying to blackout everything terrible that happened to you. But, you won't remember things. Your memory starts to become less and less, to the point where it becomes a struggle to remember it all.

You may walk around with really bad brain fog too. Abusers love to skewer your sense of reality, so when they do this, you can't remember things and your brain becomes a foggy mess as a result of this.

You Feel Constantly Guilty

One-way narcissistic abusers take you down is making you feel guilty constantly. It isn't a pity party "oh woe is me" concept, it's more of they will make you feel bad for even existing. That's the problem with narcissistic abusers. They will make sure that you feel guilty, constantly terrible, and you're the one at fault.

Narcissistic abusers will throw jabs at you, telling you how you're nothing. They will also say that you're just worthless, a piece of trash, and you're constantly not allowed to be anything more. That's the problem with many abusers. They will oftentimes make you feel guilty, to the point where depression, even suicidal tendencies start to come up.

You wonder if you're the one to blame for everything. You start to feel like you're the one at fault, when you may not be. Even when you're out of the situation and away from it, even years down the road, it can haunt you, like a ghost that hasn't been exorcised yet.

You feel bad for even being alive and that's because your narcissistic abuser has taken you to such a lower level that you don't know what to do with yourself other than to think that hey, you are the one to blame, and you are worthless.

But of course, that isn't the case.

Isolation From Help

This is what's scary about narcissistic abusers. Remember, they will claim that you're the one who is crazy, that others are lying, that you're not the one who is right here. They will tell you that you should only believe them, and never anyone else.

Over time, when you're with an abuser like this, you can develop a Stockholm syndrome, where you know that you need to get away, but you can't. you isolate yourself from help, and oftentimes, even after you get ut, you can't really get the help that you need.

That's because you don't trust other people. They are all liars, remember? Your abuser would tell you that, and even if you've managed to leave, that can hang around in your head.

That's why, when people who have been gaslighted leave their abusers, they sometimes can't trust other people. They don't know if they ever can and are scared to do so because of what their abuser did in the past.

Self-Doubt

Self-doubt stems from how you were treated by your gaslighters. The goal of those who gaslight is to make the other person feel worthless like their own thoughts and reality don't matter. Sometimes, those who have been gaslighted will hallucinate, and sometimes they'll see things that aren't there in order to make the gaslighted happy.

But, the self-doubt extends past that. When someone how has been gaslighted all their lives finally leaves, they are often scared of what's next. They've been living with the reality of their abuser for so long that they don't know how to wrench themselves away.

This causes self-doubt. It's the doubt of oneself, the doubt of what's really out there and the doubt of their own reality.

And boy is it terrible for you.

Self-doubt makes you second-guess everything that you do from here on out. After all, when you've been told you're worthless all your life, you probably will think that everything you do is worthless. But it isn't, that's just the gaslighted talking in your head.

Gaslighters love to do this because they know that, if you are continually taken down, if you ever do leave, you'll never really be yourself again, because you're scared to be. You'll be scared of expressing yourself, of being who you are, and you'll realize that, if you continue with this mindset, it will only make things worse from here on out, and for many, it can be a deadly action that can help erase who you really are.

This type of self-doubt can stifle creativity too and dreams as well, so remember that. You may feel like you should do something, but then, because you've been gaslighted in the past, you shy away from doing so. Oftentimes, this type of abuse will stunt your own creativity, and there is a reason why many people encourage those who have been gaslit to escape while they can.

Social Life Issues

Sometimes, gaslighting does affect your social life. The abuser will try their very hardest to keep the one who is gaslighted away from their friends, or even family too. The constant lying and saying they are bad people will happen. Lots of times, those who have suffered from gaslighting might end up never seeing their family until years down the road. This is something that can happen for a very long time.

What's scary as well, is that the person might end up completely isolating themselves from anyone, only relying on the abuser and nothing else. It can make the person feel like they're not capable of being loved, and also make the person feel like they're not stable, which is the scariest part about it.

For many people who have suffered the effects of gaslighting, they oftentimes will feel their confidence tank as well, since nobody seems to care about them or make an effort to go see them when in reality they're oftentimes being forced away from those relationships.

And what's scary, is that this can last a long time, even after you've left the relationship. Many who have been gaslighted in the past will not go back to their former friends and family right away, due to the effects of it. There is a reason why people will make sure that they seek out the help that they need, so they can reconnect with the person that they missed right away.

Difficulty Making Decisions

Decision Making was done all from the abuser, and not very much from the person who was gaslighted. So, if you've experienced a bit of hesitation in decisions and have a history of abuse, you can probably thank gaslighting for that.

Decisions were left to the other person, and whenever you did make decisions, it was oftentimes seen as wrong, or incorrect to do. So why make decisions then?

That's why many, who have suffered from gaslighting in the past, can doubt the decisions that they make, from there, may not believe what they're doing is right.

This can lead to anxiety disorders in many cases. You're afraid of making decisions because whenever you did, you were always told that they were wrong. You were abused so much that you don't know what to do about anything anymore, so decision making is very hard for those who've suffered from narcissistic abuse. Sometimes, this might seem like a couple of things are hard to decide, and other times, some people will just have trouble making any decision period.

Gaslighting can also make someone feel like their feelings and emotions don't matter, so they oftentimes have to choose what to do from a distanced viewpoint. So, instead of deciding from the heart, and in a way that'll validate and help you, they're swimming in a pool of anxiety and stress, that isn't fun for anyone who suffers from this.

The Mental Health Side

There is also the mental health side of the effects of gaslighting. We did go over anxiety, but that's due to the confusion that the person makes the one who is being gaslit feel. The one who is being gaslit oftentimes doesn't know what's right and wrong, and they fear to do things. This can be a small occurrence, or this can be a major issue in their life that does need to be discussed.

The one who is suffering from being gaslit may also feel a lot of hopelessness, along with self-esteem issues. This can also lead to depression, and oftentimes, people who are survivors of this oftentimes still feel like life is hopeless, that their feelings don't matter, and that they should never talk about it.

Depression is another major issue, since many times, being taken down so low for so long can make the person feel like it's not worth the energy as well.

PTSD is another one. After all, you were in a traumatic and abusive situation. The shock and stress from that person's actions still linger there, and it commonly develops from this.

Finally, codependency is something that can develop from this too. That's because you've been living a life where you had that type of relationship, and it can make you feel like you have to rely on others.

A Refusal To Show Emotions

This is a big one. This is due to the fact that survivors will always be on guard, always looking for the manipulation that's in any situation. Oftentimes, this can lead to people not trusting themselves, or trusting others either, and people do describe those who have suffered from this as always on guard.

They refuse to be vulnerable, for a good reason. They don't want to be hurt like that again. However, the problem with that, while it's a notable reason, it can be a problem for some people, since they'll refuse to show manipulation to the point where future relationships are stained, and they may have trouble holding a relationship because of this.

It does happen. Lots who suffer from this may even refuse to show emotions to others, staying single for a long time because they'd rather not be hurt, and would rather not experience what they did again.

It's a problem because they may really like someone, but the idea of being that vulnerable is something they don't think they can do, and sometimes, they will refuse to really step forward and do anything about it, and they will always keep everyone at a distance.

Some may not see this as a problem, but when the interpersonal relationships come in, it can be devastating for them.

People Pleasing

On the other side of the coin, some people will become validation hungry after they've been abused for so long. That's due to the fact that they've been forced to experience this for so long that they don't know how to do anything else but look for validation, although it may not be in the healthiest of ways.

People-pleasing isn't a good trait to have. It can make them outright refuse to change certain behaviors because they know that it pleases others. They might be seen as attention-seeking, and they will try to keep others around, even if it means sacrificing a little bit of themselves in the process.

These are the people that do harmful things to themselves, and to others, for the sole purpose of validation, but the problem is, this opens them up to further abuse. Not everyone will sympathize with the person who is recovering from abuse, and not everyone will understand. Some people will, in fact, use this person in order to further themselves. Some abusers might even go so far as to try and manipulate this person again, and from there, they become the target of another's abuse.

Abusers will look for people like this since they're incredibly easy to manipulate, they will jump right in and make this person a target. So the person who suffers from this really doesn't actively get away from the abuse, but instead, they're the subject of another abuser's attacks, whether it be someone similar or otherwise.

This is the other side of the coin, the side most people don't realize does happen if you're not careful and end up getting caught in the web of this. It can be just as bad as not showing emotion at all and tends to be worse.

That isn't to mention all of these aren't problems. They sure are, and people don't realize that if the abuse isn't taken care of or handled, it will only get harder for the person who is being gaslighted to actually break free, and do something about it. That's why many people need to understand that, in order to actively create the best situation for themselves, they need to take the abuse into their own hands and start doing something about it.

It can be very hard to escape, but it is possible. We'll talk about this. The recovery is a long road simply because the abuse basically has uncertainty at the beginning of it. People will grow up and mistrust everything that they feel, and oftentimes, recovering from this can take a long time.

But we'll tell you how to get away, and how you can use this book to escape your abuser's actions and feel better about recovering from it all.

Gaslighting at Workplace

The world of work is a competitive place. There are pressures to achieve our goals, meet deadlines, and get promoted. In this high-stress environment, it is very easy to ignore an incident of gaslighting or even continued manipulation by colleagues. Some gaslighters may be unintentionally driven to reach a once-off goal, such as achieving a promotion that you were also competing for. On a subconscious level (low level), you may wish to level the playing field if your colleague has got better qualifications than you. You may say to your colleague the morning before their interview, "Don't you think your outfit is a bit inappropriate for the position?" (And you may honestly think so.) However, your payoff is to undermine your colleague's confidence and sabotage their interview.

Gaslighting in the Home

Home is a place where we should be at peace, be able to let our guard down, and feel secure with our loved ones. Yet, it is also where we find relationships that contain narcissist traits and gaslighting. Any time that you want to make someone see something your way, you may be engaging in gaslighting. In fact, many people are "blissfully" unaware of the fact that they have been engaging in gaslighting themselves. Apart from messing around in their target's memories to instill doubt, gaslighters deny that they have acted maliciously. They will never own up to their abusive behavior unless it is to find another way to manipulate them by playing on your empathy (and sympathy).

On the low end of the spectrum, we might find a wife wanting to buy a new home entertainment center, but needing to convince her husband to do so. She may say something like, "Honey, you like this brand. Remember that you said it's a reliable brand and that you think it's worth the money? You are so right!" There may be nothing apparently abusive or manipulative about this, but when we look closer, this is a moderated example of gaslighting. The wife establishes her power by pulling the husband in with endearing terms like "honey." She then lists the virtues of the brand she likes, but she falsely indicates that the husband had been in favor of it, and how can he not remember it? She sweetens the pot by flattering the husband—he's so wise. As a result of this gaslighting, the wife gets her home theater set while also feeling victorious in convincing her husband that it was his idea to get it. However, the husband feels manipulated, and he questions his memory since he doesn't remember having said those things, but surely, he must have since his wife (whom he trusts) says that he did? He doubts himself and willingly gives his power of choice to his wife.

On the high end of the spectrum, we may find a pathological narcissist who engages in intentional gaslighting to manipulate and disempower their family and, thereby, gain strength. An example of this may be a father who acts inconsistently towards his children. One day he might tell his children off for being noisy, while tomorrow he allows them to engage in noisy behavior in the house. He then tells his children that they made a noise on both days and that he will have to punish them. The father is in a position of power and gets the thrill of punishing his children, while the children feel uncertain about what was the right thing to do as they were punished. The children may refute the father and say that he gave them permission, which he will deny by saying that he is a strict father who has always avoided his children making noise. The children will begin to doubt that they heard their father correctly and fear the results of their displeasing him.

Gaslighting in Society

On the global stage, we will find many instances of gaslighting, where people have manipulated others to achieve their goals of self-empowerment and enrichment (emotionally and financially). Certainly, politicians are renowned for it, and it comes as no surprise to most of us that they would grandstand and manipulate, so why not gaslight? What is interesting to note is that what we would consider gaslighting in one culture may not be seen as such in another. Some cultures are more susceptible to gaslighting (and narcissism) than others. Webber (2016) indicates that cultures with a more collective identity such as some African cultures, where there is an emphasis on "we" and not "I" are less likely to engage in gaslighting and narcissism as power is shared among the whole tribe or family group. In large cities, there is also more pressure on people to reach individual excellence, which will encourage gaslighting, than in smaller towns or out in the rural countryside.On the lower end of the scale, people worldwide will engage in gaslighting when it suits them and to attain a specific goal. They may do so to discipline and control their children by, for example, telling their child that they really do like going to school when the child hates it. The upper reaches of the scale for gaslighting globally may be best captured by referring to historical figures such as Hitler and Mussolini. They went from gaslighting (as Hitler did with his propaganda and speeches to draw in the crowds and convincing them of truths that they knew were false) before ending in a dictatorship. When looking at the strategies that Hitler used to gain prominence in German politics before World War II, it reads like the three stages of narcissist manipulations (or gaslighting) with Hitler wooing the people (idealization) and promising them everything their hearts desired, before suddenly changing to persecutions (devaluation), and, finally, death camps (discard). Granted, not all narcissists will engage in gaslighting to the point of being equivalent to Hitler; however, we may find the whole spectrum of emotional abuse in our lives if we look closely.

How to Reduce Conflicts in Relationships

Being in touch with your feelings and emotions can be an important way to protect yourself from future abuse. We are doomed to repeat history if we choose not to learn from it. It can be necessary to take a long hard look at your own needs to determine if you are capable of having these needs met within your current relationship. Self-reflection requires honesty. Honesty can be painful, but it is through this pain that we are able to complete a metamorphosis.

This tactic of manipulation can keep victims glued to an abuser's side. Self-love can be a powerful wedge, allowing the abused partner to become the comfort that they're so desperately seeking from the abuser. No matter the outcome, staying or leaving, we must learn to care for ourselves. A person who doesn't value themselves will accept demeaning and degrading behavior because they feel as though they deserve it.

You deserve to be happy. Your situation may feel absolutely hopeless, but I can promise you that you have it within yourself to make any decision you need to in the interest of self-preservation. Admitting to yourself that you're in an abusive relationship can feel a bit like taking a step toward the edge of a cliff that drops into oblivion, an unknown abyss. You know that you are comfortable in this misery, but this isn't happiness.

Taking these next steps takes courage. It takes bravery that I know you have because you are reading this book. Because you have been researching and allowing the thoughts to turn over and over again in your mind. You can absolutely do this, even when it feels utterly hopeless. Even if you are completely dependent upon the abusive partner.

Forgiveness

This isn't forgiveness for abuse; that will come later. This is an honest look at the relationship. It is imperative to understand that, as a victim of abuse, you participated in this situation. There is something inside that has been ashamed and afraid to take any ownership of this hardship. Listen, you have wounds that you will need to heal.

There are reasons that you gravitated toward an abusive partner, and that is something that will need to be addressed one day. For now, forgiveness.

You are worthy of attention, love, and kindness. Begin to manifest these things by caring for yourself. Understand that you had a hand in this dynamic and forgive yourself. This is the first step toward trusting yourself again. There are so many ways to process the guilt that we feel in these situations, and you can choose what works for you. Reflection is enough for some, but others find it helpful to write yourself a letter.

Invest in Yourself

Abusive relationships have the potential to rob us of our confidence. Narcissistic partners want you to feel as though you are silly and irrelevant, and your goals do not matter. It is much easier to lord over another person if their spirit is broken. Loving one's self can be the most difficult thing in the world when it feels like everything is against you. Any normal human being dropped in a situation such as this is miserable and dejected.

Make a plan to begin gluing the shattered pieces of yourself back together. This sounds like a huge and abstract undertaking, but it doesn't have to be.

Learning to love yourself again can be as familiar as coming home to an old friend. We are going to take it step by step.

Human beings are uniquely cognizant, which affords us a measure of control over our own lives that the rest of the animal kingdom is missing. Situations (like abusive relationships) can force us into a fishbowl and take away this control. It can be so easy to overlook that we can be exactly what we want to be. We can make it so easy to love ourselves by becoming our own hero. Be the sort of person that you would love and admire.

Make a list of the qualities and values that you want to embody. List goals and milestones that you want to achieve. It can help if you close your eyes and picture a person that you really admire; this person can be a role model or someone that you have completely made up. What makes this person so admirable to you? Independence? Bravery? Fashion sense? There is nothing too silly.

You are authoring the next changes that will occur in your own life. This list may have as many entries as you need. The following is an example to use as a template, should you become stumped:

Who I want to Be:

- Creative
- Funny
- Brave

This list is a way for you to take back your self-image from your abusive partner's hands. It is your job to decide who you want to be. You decide what you value, your hair color, your goals, and the way that you handle conflict. You don't have to see yourself through the eyes of someone who is incentivized to keep you down.

Now that you have created your list, break it down entry by entry. This is going to be a map to achieving your goals. Working on your list will give you a project to focus on when the days become dark, and it is a fast-track way to relearn self-love. Creating these lists also inches us closer and closer to self-reliance. Each individual goal from your list is now a new list, with steps that you can take to achieve these things. Example:

Creative:

- Research different creative mediums.
- Buy the sketchbook or supplies needed to begin learning new skills.
- Use art to express anger or sadness.
- Experiment with other methods.

There is no goal or quality that cannot be broken down in this way. Take the pen back from your partner and begin writing your own story again. Stimulate these healthy conversations with yourself, because this communication is going to be necessary moving forward.

Find an Outlet

In order to protect yourself from bottling up the words of an abusive partner, it can be important to find an outlet to use for self-expression. Journaling could be a great way to document the abuse and rise above it. There is a lot of unreleased tension in victims of abuse. Stress and anxiety have become a staple of everyday life. Any moment might bring another fight.

Vent your anger or sadness through a journal or other artistic medium. Allow your mind to rant and rave about the things that you are feeling. Having a way to relieve some of the pressure can be vital in abuse cases. It can also be helpful to find an interest to focus on and is a great way to learn a new skill.

Research Research Research

In the same way that you bought this book, begin obsessively consuming material about narcissists, codependents, or abuse. There is a certain mystery to the way that our brains work in these situations. Sometimes we can be unsure of our own actions and motivations. In order to heal, it is necessary to understand.

Demystifying abuse will allow you to pull back the veil shrouding the abuser. The only way that you are going to believe that your partner has something wrong is if you are faced with the facts over and over again. Learn the patterns of abuse and clinical definitions.

Absorbing articles, videos, books, and other literature on the subject will also allow you to predict your partner's next moves. The abusive partner may seem erratic and unpredictable, but there are reasons behind every behavior. Every name that you have ever been called out of malice.

Both narcissists and codependents require validation in the same way. This validation is achieved through manipulation and sometimes name-calling and random fights. A narcissist can seem loving one moment and vile the next, but this is just another part of their process.

Learn everything that you can while you are trapped in this situation. Anticipate the attack and allow the words to roll right off of your skin. When you understand the motivation, then the fights stop seeming so personal.

Exercise

Eating and living in a sedentary way is often related to depression and stress. Take back your wellbeing by taking care of your body. This will help improve the way that you feel physically and your self-esteem. Exercise will also help fight all the negative emotions with the brain chemicals that it produces. Exercising for just thirty minutes a day can drastically allow you to change the way that you see yourself. Abuse will slowly and deviously steal away your confidence and happiness.

Exercise is recommended by doctors to treat both anxiety and depression. Endorphins are released that encourage an overall calm that can combat feelings of negativity brought on by your surroundings. The movement can also induce a meditative state that allows you to forget about the troubles that await you when you return home.

Challenge Your Comfort Zone

When your life feels stale, prison-like, and depressing, it can be difficult to spring back to life. Challenging yourself to escape this comfort zone is hard, but it can also be a very rewarding experience. There are so many volunteer organizations that would love to have assistance. Social activities of this nature may also allow you to find new friends and reestablish a support system.

Your partner will object to these ventures, especially if they are narcissistic. It can be a good idea to shrug off their watchful eye and do some activities that you are interested in. If you are concerned that they will be angry when they find you, remember that they are angry (for sport) constantly anyway. There is no winning, so you might as well take care of your own needs.

Self-soothing

Break free of the abusive trauma bond by becoming the person that you turn to for your own comfort. Do not allow your partner to take away the pain of a fresh fight by becoming a different person right in front of you. Learn tactics to calm yourself down, as this talent has the potential to save you from the bondage of an abusive relationship.

When you need to calm yourself, use cozy blankets in a quiet room. Read a book until your body feels less stressed. Listen to relaxing music or play a podcast to drift along on the tone of a stranger's voice. Sometimes it can even be helpful to just allow yourself to feel the anger and sadness and then go about your day.

Baths are a wonderful way to calm down. Candles can also be helpful. Learn about the things that work to relax you and reach for those the next time you are upset. Abusive partners will dangle comfort over your head so that you bend to their will. Behaviors like this make a narcissist feel powerful. Learn to be your own hero and your own light in the dark.

Praise Yourself

If you are dating a narcissist, then your self-image has been ripped to shreds. The narcissist is doing this for their own gain. Their view of you has nothing to do with who you actually are. Begin to shake off all that negative and toxic commentary and challenge yourself to replace it with words of encouragement. There are so many areas where you excel. You have so many brilliant ideas. You are so resilient.

Next time your partner is calling you names or mocking you, pretend that they are doing these things to a friend.

You would tell that person that the abuser was all wrong and that they are worthy of love. Treat yourself with the same respect.

Stop the Comparison

Comparing yourself to others can add another layer of toxicity on an already toxic sandwich. Your relationship isn't good right now, and there is no need to hold yourself up to someone who has it together at the moment. You are learning some of the most important lessons of your life, and it is already difficult.

Spending too much time on social media can damage your confidence further. Avoid the things that do not make you feel good. Your journey is completely different from those around you. You are dealing with a situation that many people would not be strong enough to make it through.

Time for Yourself

In order to maintain your sanity in the chaos around you, it is necessary for you to spend time doing the things that you love. Music, swimming, hiking, or dancing would all be great examples of activities that allow for escape and relaxation.

It is imperative that you keep your relationship from defining your life.

Your partner may object to you spending time without them around because they would rather you not have the chance to calm down. For your own sanity, do whatever you need to do to go out on your own without your partner. There need to be boundaries set that your partner will not cross.

Activities that allow for reflection can also be a good idea. Meditation and yoga will help to solidify your overall mental health.

Learning to keep your center in the face of chaos can be a useful skill to have in these situations.

Therapy

It is not always easy to get to a therapist when you are in an abusive relationship. A professional is going to be the best way to seek help for yourself. Therapy will also allow you to reclaim your sanity and stolen self-esteem. A professional will be able to offer you guidance tailored to your specific situation.

Talking to a professional is the quickest and most effective way to address your mental state and the condition of your relationship.

The therapist will be able to help you see your situation in an objective way. This can also help to restore your self-worth.

Is There Anything to Save?

Use these same eyes to look at your partner. Make a list of qualities that you require in a mate or in a relationship. Things that are important to your overall happiness and wellbeing. Do you want independence within your relationship? Do you want a partner who doesn't lash out in anger?

Objectively, if you are making no excuses for anyone else's behavior, can your partner be the person that you need them to be? Have you been looking at this relationship in rose-colored glasses? Do not allow fleeting moments of kindness to obscure mountains of bad behavior.

Codependency is a deeply rooted behavior that can take lots of effort to change. To save a relationship that is plagued with codependency, both partners must be willing to take steps to change their behavior. Therapy is likely going to be necessary because personal accountability is lacking from the side of the controlling partner. You know your partner better than anyone else, and it is going to take so much honesty to be able to move forward in a way that benefits both parties.

Empathy is the deciding factor. Has your partner ever done anything for you without expecting repayment? Do you believe that your partner is attached to you, or the things that you are able to do for them? These questions are also dependent on the level of control that your partner is exerting upon, because if abuse is involved beyond manipulation, then you need to leave.

If you are involved with a partner that you suspect is a narcissist, things will not change. Empathy is necessary for the relationship to evolve into something that isn't harmful toward both parties. There are extenuating circumstances (such as shared children) that force some victims to continue relationships with narcissist partners. Extensive therapy is needed to keep the abusive partner in check, and these situations involve the victim forgoing a healthy romantic relationship.

Unless children are involved (and usually even if children are involved), the most sensible course of action is to go. Narcissists panic when they have been threatened with being alone. They will not move on until they have found someone that they consider to better. These individuals will pretend that they are going to change their behavior to save the relationship; they may even believe this.

The fact of the matter is that narcissism is a slow poison. Most psychologists that this disorder is incurable and will be a detriment to anyone close to the abuser.

A narcissist will promise change. Their behavior will get better for a few weeks or maybe even a month. They may even want to save the partnership. It isn't possible for these partners to act in opposition to their nature for very long, and their nature is to serve themselves through the oppression of those closest to them. If you are in the blast-zone, then you are always at risk.

How to Know When it's Time to Go

For those in narcissistic relationships, this research is likely a sign that the end is drawing near. You have probably made up your mind already when it comes to the dissolution of your relationship. Most readers of this book are either retroactively reading about their experience or are entering the miserable stage of limbo right before the trigger is pulled. A stage of stagnation where you are left wondering if you will ever find the courage to say the words.

If you are teetering on the edge of singledom, listening to your own body can be a clue to your deeper desires.

Do you still enjoy spending time with your partner? Do you dread being in the same room with your significant other? What does your body tell you about time spent together?

If there is any physical violence in your relationship, the time to go is now or the soonest that you can safely escape. When you are caught in a cycle of abuse, it can be best to make up your mind and wait silently for an opportunity to run. The best thing that you can do for your future is to guard your safety now. Leaving is a provocation and should be done swiftly and quietly. Have people in your life on standby, ready to assist you with your escape when you give the word.

Readers who are involved in codependent relationships must assure that their partner is willing and capable of change. If the offending party is comfortable with the dynamic of the partnership, this is a strong indication that nothing will change. Never feel guilty for taking steps to ensure your own happiness. You are not responsible for the feelings of others. Threats and further attempts at manipulation are a good sign that you are making the right choice.

Those who leave partners who have controlled and belittled them throughout the relationship have this deeply ingrained view that they are unworthy of love. Victims believe that if they leave such a situation, no one else would want them.

Their hobbies, interests, values, and looks have been torn apart for so long that it can be hard for them to see themselves as worthy.

The fights are always manipulated to seem as though the victim is deserving of the abuse. The victim made a tiny mistake, so the abuser is justified in exploding. No matter what the victim does, it will never be enough to stop the flood. If you have found yourself asking your partner to stop criticizing your every move, you may be one of these victims. Do you believe that you have been treated like a partner should be treated? If the answer is no, then it is time to formulate a plan.

How to Recognize Manipulation and Take Back Control

There will be many challenges that you will face, but in the long run, you will be in a better position. Many people struggle with how lonely it is after divorcing their partner. We are going to look over how you can overcome loneliness so that you do not get sucked back into a relationship with your ex.

Obviously, when you do start looking at getting into a new relationship, it is going to be extremely scary. It will likely take quite a while for you to truly open up and trust someone again. We're also going to look at what you can do to make sure that you are choosing a partner that is going to be healthy for you. Included in this, we will give you narcissistic traits to watch out for, so you don't end up making the same mistakes twice. Most people learn the lesson fairly quickly about what to avoid after being with a narcissist, but the more information you have the better off you will be.

Trust is going to be extremely difficult for you. It will take time for you to be able to open up and allow someone into your heart. This is completely normal as you have suffered mass devastation at the hands of someone who was supposed to love you. Make sure you are being patient with yourself. There is no rush. If you are having worries about entering into a relationship or trusting another person, it may be a clear sign that you're not quite ready to date again, and that is completely OK.

We discussed how to go about healing from your narcissistic marriage. We also went over the process of moving on and the struggles that you may face. Letting go can be extremely hard when your relationship has been your sole focus for a long amount of time. Know that with perseverance, strength, and education, you will be able to come back and lead a healthy and fulfilling life that is free from the abuse of a narcissist.

Overcoming Loneliness

Regardless of if you were married to a narcissist or not, when you divorce someone, it is going to lead to feelings of loneliness. These feelings can be almost debilitating; they are so strong. Unfortunately, extreme loneliness could encourage you to go back to your toxic relationship so that you simply aren't alone. Obviously, this is something you should avoid at all costs, especially if you just divorced a narcissist.

Divorce can feel very isolating. When you divorce a narcissist, it can be even more so as they will likely do their best to turn everyone against you. You must remember that you are absolutely not alone and that there are a plethora of people that are working through the same hardships that you are. You must also remember that there are at least some people that can see your ex-spouse for who they are and will be ready to stand by your side at a moment's notice.

One great way to help you move on and combat the loneliness that comes from divorce is to join support groups that can help you work your way through it. You don't have to do this in the public eye if you don't feel ready as there are many online support groups that are available to help you heal and move past everything that has happened to you. These types of groups help you feel a sense of inclusion, and it can help combat the loneliness that you are currently experiencing.

A lot of the loneliness that you may be feeling could be due to the fact that you are isolating yourself. This is a common thing to happen once you have left a narcissistic relationship, as you will likely be working through a variety of different issues. Let's look at a three-step system that can help you get past your loneliness and isolation.

The first step is to allow yourself plenty of time to grieve. The grieving process can be quite lengthy, and it feels as if you are on an emotional rollercoaster. This makes many people want to speed past the grieving process, but it won't be beneficial if you do. The more you try to speed up the grieving process, the more you will actually be lengthening it. You should also be aware that you should avoid rushing into a new relationship. New relationships right after divorce may postpone the grieving process, but it will not stop it altogether. You really do need to allow yourself to grieve over the harm that has come to you and the loss of your marriage.

The next step is to not allow yourself to focus on the past longer than you need to. As you are grieving and healing, you will definitely need to spend some time looking over past experiences, but once you have accepted them and you understand them, you need to move on.

When you are constantly looking at the past, it can actually increase the loneliness, sadness, and anger that you feel. You are absolutely entitled to all of the negative feelings that you have experienced from your past, but if you hold on to them for a long amount of time, it can be very difficult to completely move on and find the ability to enjoy your life. You must always remember that the relationship you had with the narcissist is a thing of the past and life will improve as long as you dedicate yourself to healing.

The last step is to not be afraid to reach out for help. When you are trying to work through the pain that has been caused to you and the extreme heartache that you are feeling, a solid support system is exactly the right answer.

The people in life that are not afraid to reach out for help always seem to find a way to land on their feet. Choosing to try and do it alone tends to add to the suffering that an individual will feel. Additionally, it lengthens the time that you will feel extremely lonely and lost. Whether you choose to find support from friends, family members, therapists, or support groups, there is no wrong decision. In fact, the more people you have in your corner to help support you through this arduous journey, the better off you are.

Reaching out for support is probably one of the most important pieces when you are trying to shake the loneliness that comes after divorce. When we connect with other people that understand us and understand the situation that we have come from, it makes it easier to break free of isolation. There are some fabulous retreats and other activities that you can participate in with people that have similar experiences, and it can be extremely freeing.

Choosing a New Partner

Now that we have looked at a variety of ways to help you shed the loneliness factor, we want to discuss choosing a new partner and starting to date again. This can be utterly terrifying due to the fact that you were fooled once, and you will never want to be fooled in that way again. There are a lot of different things that you will need to learn, but there are also things that you will need to unlearn after being the victim of narcissistic abuse.

More often than not, people that have suffered from the hands of someone that has a personality disorder will want to learn about it.

Obviously, knowledge is power, so learning about personality disorders can help keep you safe from falling into a relationship with someone that has one.

You must understand that there are varying degrees of personality disorders and just because someone has 1 does not mean that they will not be a suitable fit for you. However, recognizing the signs of a serious personality disorder that will cause you to harm is a good way to ensure that you don't go back through the torture that was being in a relationship with a narcissist.

Not only will you have to learn a variety of different things before being comfortable stepping into a new relationship, but you are also going to need to unlearn some things. The narcissist in your life probably did a pretty good job at twisting and warping your reality. Undoing the damage that they have done will take time, but it is completely possible. You will likely need to take a step back from yourself and look at each experience with the narcissist individually so that you can see the truth of what actually happened. It is quite likely that you have already worked through that process if you are considering looking for a new partner at all.

Deciding to date after leaving a narcissistic relationship is something that can be extremely difficult as it can take years to truly heal and work through all of the obstacles that come along with narcissistic abuse. Don't be afraid to discuss what is on your mind with your friends, family, and therapist. It is fairly likely that your thoughts and ideas about love and relationships are still a little bit skewed and getting other's opinions on the situation can make it clearer as to what the right choice for you is.

When you are starting to consider dating again, you should take the time to brush up on the red flags that help you easily see that someone is a narcissist. You should also take the time to remember what your relationship with the narcissist was like in the beginning. More often than not, the beginning is a time that felt positive with your ex and examining it can show you some of the early signs pinpointing a person as a narcissist.

Let's take a look at a variety of different red flags that try to clue you in that someone is a narcissist. If you see these traits in someone you are considering dating, you are better off to run for the Hills rather than think it is a fluke or that you can change them.

One of the first red flags that you should watch out for is people that have a showy, flashy, or larger than life attitude. If you would make this statement about someone that you have never met anyone like them or it's like they are a magnet, you should be leery. If you genuinely like someone, you will be able to explain what it is about them that you like. So, the inability to explain what it is that draws you to a person is a red flag that they may not be relationship material.

Another huge red flag is when someone expresses their love for you after a short amount of time. If you have not been dating someone for very long, you should be concerned if they are committing themselves to you. It takes time for love and serious feelings to develop, so if you see that somebody is rushing in and telling you that they love you quickly, it is a pretty good clue that it will lead to an unhealthy relationship.

Love bombing is another major red flag that you absolutely need to pay attention to. If someone is showing you in an overwhelming amount of adoration or attraction without a core that is emotional, you should be concerned. Many narcissists use love bombing to manipulate and gain control over a person. It is actually quite surprising how often it works. If an alarm bell is setoff inside of you because someone is paying you an overwhelming amount of attention, you should listen to what your intuition is telling you and stay away from that person.

All of us have at least a few stories about our crazy ex-relationships. If the person you are interested in only has stories that are negative or expresses that they have only been in relationships that are toxic, you should see this as a red flag. More often than not, when people talk this way about their past relationships, they will take no accountability for the problems that or present. As you know, narcissists are unable to take responsibility or accountability for their actions, so if they don't have any positive things to say about the previous relationships, and you need to distance yourself from them right away.

The last red flag can easily be observed if you sit back and take a look at how your prospective partner treats other people. Pay attention to how he treats waiters and waitresses at restaurants. You should also take notice of how they speak about the opposite sex. If they show disrespect for those around them, it can be a great warning sign that you are dealing with a narcissist.

This is a pretty decent look at the different red flags that you need to get familiar with to determine whether or not your prospective mate is a narcissist. There are a plethora of different traits that you may witness.

The best thing you can do to ensure that you don't end up in another relationship with a narcissist is to be mindful of your experiences. Try and stay present at the moment so that you have a good understanding of what is actually transpiring in front of you.

Making sure that you are connected with your mind, body, and soul will also help you avoid entering into another narcissistic relationship. There is a massive amount of intuition stored inside of us. When we learn to listen to what our bodies are telling us, it can seriously help us avoid the negative consequences of getting into a toxic relationship.

Getting in touch with your inner self is not a difficult process, but it will take a bit of time. Most people find that meditation is one of the best ways to find that connection and provide yourself with the ability to interpret what your body is telling you. Your subtle body will notice red flags and negative traits in a person well before your conscious mind will be able to. This makes it pretty easy to see why connecting with yourself is so important in making sure that you are choosing a healthy person to be in a relationship with.

You should always keep in mind that intuition works in both directions.

It can alert you when you are in a situation or around a person that is unsafe, and it can also clue you in when you are in front of a great match. When you are in tune with your body, recognizing the signals that it provides you with is relatively easy. You then simply need to remember to listen to what it is saying.

When you are in a relationship with a narcissist, it tends to do a lot of damage to a person's sense of reality and sense of self. You may not be able to easily recognize your personal feelings, preferences, or even your own opinions after leaving a narcissist. So, you will need to spend a lot of time reflecting on who you actually are. As you sit back and remember the things that you like and the things that you enjoy, you will start to remember who you actually are. You have to let go of the manipulation that was used to change all of your opinions so that they matched the desires of the narcissist.

When you are trying to reclaim your life, it is incredibly important that you take the time to remember who you are. There is no preference too small for a narcissist to try and change so, relearning all of the things about you that you used to know may be a difficult task, but it is necessary so that you can move on.

One of the best ways to find your true self and reconnect with your true thoughts, feelings, and ideas is to meditate and ask yourself some very basic questions. You want to ask yourself things like:

- What are the things that I truly enjoy doing?
- What things in life Do I dislike?
- What is my favorite food?
- Which season is my favorite?
- What is my favorite color?
- What are the things in life that I am truly good at?

These are only a few examples of the basic questions that you should start to ask yourself so that you can re-identify the person that you truly are. It may seem ridiculous to ask yourself such basic questions, but realistically, your narcissistic abuser could have easily warped your opinions so that they matched their own personal thoughts. It is really quite amazing how many things you can rediscover about yourself once you have stepped away from the narcissistic abuser that was in your life.

Creating a Healthy Relationship

Creating and maintaining a healthy relationship is not quite as hard as everyone makes it out to be. If you have suffered from narcissistic abuse, you may have very little faith in the fact that you can enter in and sustain a healthy relationship. It is totally normal to feel this way, but if you take the time to grieve and heal, eventually, you'll be able to see that healthy relationships are not a thing of fallacy.

We are going to look over the different elements that will help you create a healthy and long-lasting relationship. Some of these things are quite basic, but they're also extremely important. It is very likely that the things on this list will all be the opposite of what you have experienced while in a relationship with a narcissist.

This can make it hard to believe, but somewhere inside of you, you will know that it is true.

One of the first steps in creating a healthy relationship is to learn how to love yourself. When you are comfortable with the person that you are, you will lead a happier life, and this will impact your relationship in a positive way. Learning how to love yourself after experiencing narcissistic abuse takes time and patience.

However, as you rediscover yourself and learn how to accept the experience of narcissistic abuse and move on from it, loving yourself will become easier.

Communication is one of the most prevalent linchpins in creating a positive and healthy relationship. Many people struggle when trying to communicate with their partners, but you need to keep trying. Don't be afraid to ask questions and always take the time to listen to what your partner has to say. If emotions become heightened and you are not in control of them, there is nothing wrong with taking time to compose yourself. Simply let your partner know that you need to put a pin in the conversation and assure them you will come back to it later. On that note, make sure to come back to it later. When we communicate with our partner about everything that is happening with us, it helps to increase the amount of trust that both parties have in each other, and it strengthens the bond of the relationship. Remember to not always focus on the negative but to communicate about the positive as well.

Alongside communication comes honesty. It is unfortunate how difficult being honest is for some people. There are definitely times that telling the truth may be hurtful to your partner, but it is always going to be better than telling them lies. Lies cause more damage in a relationship than pretty much everything else.

You will truly learn how to trust somebody with your whole self when both parties are being open and honest about everything that is going on in their lives.

Another thing that needs to happen to ensure that you are creating a healthy relationship is to remember that both people involved in it need space. It is not healthy for you to spend every minute of your time together. Sure, it is likely that you will spend a lot of time together, but you should also make time to enjoy your own friends and participate in the activities you enjoy outside of your relationship. Distance does help the heart grow fonder, so taking time for yourself will only make things better between you and your mate.

You should also never be afraid to agree to disagree about the issues that you are facing. As individuals, we all have our own opinions and ideas. You don't need to see eye to eye about everything that is discussed between the two of you. Instead, be respectful of your partner's thoughts and opinions, and in return, they need to be respectful of yours.

Another element that can help ensure that you have a healthy relationship is finding the ability to forgive and to ask for forgiveness. No one is perfect, and we all make mistakes.

 Don't be afraid to take accountability and apologize for the things that you have done wrong, your partner will appreciate your honesty, and it will help improve the level of trust between the two of you. Additionally, you need to understand that your partner is going to make mistakes as well. You need to be willing to hear them and accept when they apologize to you for their mistakes.

This is only a look at the many things you can do to make sure that your relationship stays healthy and that it is good for both parties involved. You should continuously check in with your partner and inquire about their thoughts and feelings, as this helps to show that you care. Be mindful and patient with not only yourself but also with your partner. Kindness goes a long way.

How to Deal with A Person with A Border Personality Disorder

In general, people with BPD do not want special treatment. They just wished to be loved; an emotion which, thanks to traumatic upbringings, they may never have truly experienced. For BPDs simple things such as maintain friendships or cohabiting can be enormous challenges.

People with BPD exhibit heightened levels of sensitivity, meaning even the smallest criticism can cause great offense, leading them to behave with aggression and hostility. In addition, they are prone to misconstruing things that are said to them and taking offense when none was intended.

These factors can make relating to someone with borderline personality disorder a complete minefield. While you want to treat your loved one the same way you would others, you must also be aware of the erratic behavior their disorder can cause.

Here are few ways to speak to and relate to a friend, partner or family member suffering from BPD:

What to Do:

- Ensure your meaning is as clear as possible. Do not rely on subtleties or facial expressions to get your meaning across.
- Offer ongoing and regular support. Listen to them, offer assistance and comfort when needed.

- Validate what they are going through. Acknowledge that, while you may not be able to relate to their experience, you understand it is very real to them.
- If you understand the way they are feeling, tell them. But if their feelings do not make sense to you, try to find out more. Ask questions. Let them know you really want to understand. Encourage them to tell you more about the things they are feeling and why.
- Give them hope by acknowledging that other sufferers of BPD have gone on to live long and happy lives.
- Acknowledge that the person is suffering and help them break their goals down into small, manageable steps.
- Have realistic expectations. The nature of BPD means setbacks are commonplace. Do your best to remain positive and encourage the person to do the same.
- If it is appropriate, ask them about their BPD management plan and find out what role you can play in implementing this.
- Communicate your boundaries clearly. Tell them what you are not prepared to accept, be it abusive language, violence, threats, etc.
- If they are agitated, do your best to respond in a calm manner. If you feel in danger, remove yourself from the situation and call for help.
- Listening and reflecting on what you have been told is perhaps the most effective way of communicating with someone with BPD. Even though you may disagree with every word that comes out of your loved one's

mouth, acknowledge that listening is not the same as agreeing to someone. You are simply accepting the person's emotions and perspective.

- Ask open-ended questions that encourage your loved one to share pieces of their life, such as "Tell me what happened today to make you feel like this?" or "How is your week going?"

- Summarizing back what you have been told. This helps someone with BPD feel heard and valued. For example, if your partner shares that she thinks you don't love her as much as you used to, you could say, "All right, you feel that I don't love you as much as I used to." Again, by doing this, you are not agreeing with the statement, you are simply acknowledging the emotions and perspective of the other person. Avoid the temptation to point out all the flaws in the argument remind yourself that the goal of this reflection is not necessarily to agree. It is not about proving who is right or wrong. It is about helping someone you love to feel valued and heard, and about de-escalating conflict before it transmutes into a crisis.

- Focus on emotions, not words. BPD sufferers are prone to speaking in ways that may come across as hurtful or antagonistic, and it can be difficult not to focus on these words. But rather than pulling your loved one up on something they may have said, look beneath their words to the core emotion beneath. If you sense your loved one is struggling, ask questions such as: "It seems as though you are feeling hurt right now, is that right?"

Asking questions such as these will validate your loved one and their feelings and help them feel as though they are being heard.

What Not to Do:

- Do not attempt to take control of a person's life. Allow them to make their own choices and simply offer your support. Do not let this become a source of conflict.
- Avoid being drawn into their conflicts with other people. Do not be drawn into their attempts to do so.
- Do not try and talk them out of their feelings. A BPD sufferer might come to you with a claim like "I am a terrible person." Flat out disagreeing with this with a comment like: "You're not a terrible person," has the effect of invalidating their thoughts and feelings. Instead, try to understand what it is that has made them feel this way. Ask questions and listen carefully. Find out if there was something specific they did to make them feel like a terrible person. From there, engage in practical problem-solving – ask them what they can do to rectify the situation. Doing so gives the BPD sufferer a sense of being in control of their own lives and emotions.
- Do not attempt to be their therapist. Instead, assist your loved one in finding the right healthcare professional for them and offer your support throughout their treatment.
- Do not get defensive. While it can be challenging not to take accusations and criticisms personally,

acknowledge that it is not about you. This is just a manifestation of the BPD. Remind yourself of this on a regular basis and do your best to see beyond the illness to the person you love beneath.

How to Communicate effectively during a crisis

When a loved one is in the midst of a BPD episode, they may become aggressive, insult you or hurl out unfair accusations. As humans, our natural response is to become defensive and counter their arguments with hostility and aggression of our own. But when dealing with a BPD sufferer, acting such a way will only exacerbate the situation. It is important to remember that someone with BPD finds it difficult to see things from someone else's perspective. They have difficulty telling the difference between a minor issue and a full-blown catastrophe. When you behave defensively, they see this as a sign that they are not valued. This will lead them to believe that you do not want to be around them, triggering their deep-seated fear of abandonment. This then leads them to act recklessly or in a self-harming manner.

Instead, when your loved ones become reactive, take time to pay attention to what they are saying, without pointing out the holes in their argument. While it is easier said than done, do your best not to take their attack personally. After all, it is not about you. If your loved one makes a point about something you did wrong or something you could improve on in the future, acknowledge and accept their point, make your apology, and attempt to discuss ways you can improve in the future. When someone with BPD feels as though they are being heard and taken seriously, the situation is less likely to get out of hand. If, however, if the conflict increases to points of threats, aggression or a tantrum, it will be most beneficial to walk away and attempt the conversation again when they have calmed down.

How to Identify an Emergency

While disparaging self-talk is a common feature of borderline personality disorder, particular among those suffering from 'quiet' BPD, the sad reality is self-harming and suicide is all too common among people suffering from this disorder. When you are around a person with BPD, it is important to be vigilant and aware of any attempts at self-harming that may be taking place. When someone with BPD is reactive, it can easily escalate to the point where they will consider self-harming. It is important, however, not to plant the idea of self-injury or suicide in their head by outwardly asking them if they are considering it. Instead, provide a space where they can speak openly about what it is they are feeling or experiencing. This will then allow you to make a decision about whether to seek professional help on that occasion.

Be aware that there are several subtle signs that may indicate a person is considering suicide or engaging in self-harm. These include shaving off their hair, isolating themselves from others, excessive scratching or a reduced appetite. These less overt symptoms represent the BPD sufferer's inability to discuss their emotions outwardly. Being alert to these symptoms and seeking help accordingly can stop a crisis from escalating and requiring serious psychiatric or medical attention.

All suicide and self-harming attempts should be taken seriously. Even if they are done to seek attention, they are still indicative of deep emotional trauma. While it is important to get your loved one professional assistance in any situation involving self-harm and suicide, seek help immediately if any of the following occurs:

- The person has deliberately injured themselves.
- The person is expressing suicidal thoughts or talking about killing someone else
- The person is acting in an aggressive and abusive manner
- The person has become disoriented; i.e. they do not know who they are, where they are, or what day it is.
- The person has become delusional or is having hallucinations
- The person has become severely affected by drugs and/or alcohol and is acting in a reckless manner.

If you don't believe the situation has escalated to the point of being life-threatening, however, refraining from calling the emergency services. Doing so every time your loved one speaks of hurting themselves will signal to them that they have a great amount of power over you and that by threatening to self-harm, they can effectively put an end to any conflict or argument. Instead, when your loved one speaks about self-harming, ask them what they would like to do about the situation. Suggest calling their therapist or an emergency hotline or going together to the emergency room. Doing this gives the BPD sufferer back an element of control, which can assist in calming their runaway emotions.

What to Do When You Feel Overwhelmed

There is no doubt that having a loved one with BPD is a struggle. There are bound to be times when you feel overwhelmed and unable to cope. This is exacerbated by the fact that the person you love with BPD will generally be unable to fulfill the supportive role of parent, a friend or partner than they otherwise would.

Because of this, it is crucial to have a strong network around you of people you can rely on in times of exhaustion, stress and overwhelm. Allow yourself plenty of time to engage in hobbies and relaxation activities with friends who you can be open with. Ensure too that you have people you can speak openly to about the experience of living with someone with a borderline personality disorder. This may be a therapist or other health professional, a support group, GP or religious leader.

Involving other people in your support and care of the BPD sufferer can also be invaluable. Caring for someone with a mental illness should never fall to one person alone. Ensure there are a number of people around you who are well-versed in dealing with the individual with BPD and are able to act calmly and rationally in times of crisis. The more people around the BPD sufferer who know effective strategies for dealing with their reactivity, the less likely it is that a crisis will occur. Depending on the situation, your loved one's friends, siblings, parents, children or extended family members are all people who can be turned to for support.

Manage your expectations with regards to recovery

When dealing with a physical illness, recovery is often very black and white. But recovery is completely different when it comes to mental illness. Very rarely does recovery see the complete elimination of symptoms and it is unlikely that someone suffering from a mental health disorder will ever be able to completely dispense with the need for therapy, medication or other treatments. When dealing with a borderline personality disorder, recovery can be measured in a number of ways.

A sufferer in recovery will experience less frequent emotional outbursts, and these outbursts will decrease in intensity. There will be fewer incidences of self-harming and other impulsive, reckless behavior. While it is, of course, possible that there will be relapses, such crises will likely be resolved much more quickly than in the past. As their symptoms improve, your loved one will likely feel more and more confident taking steps towards living a full and successful life. Offering your support at every step of the journey will go a long way towards assisting this recovery.

Being in a Relationship with Someone with BPD

Often, people with BPD are very charismatic and energetic, so it is not difficult to be drawn to them. For this reason, many people find themselves in relationships with sufferers of borderline personality disorder. But the challenges of this illness mean a relationship with such a person is likely to be a cycle of perpetual arguments and dramas.

But while conducting a relationship with someone with BPD can be a challenge, if you have found a partner whom you love and care for, the relationship is likely worth pursuing. The key lies in knowing what to expect, and how your partner's disorder may manifest itself.

Understanding Your Partner

To really understand what is going on inside your partner's head, ensure you have read Part One of this book; a detailed overview of borderline personality disorder, its causes and the ways it can manifest. But here are a few of the traits of BPD that can be most prominent within a romantic relationship.

As people with BPD have such difficulty controlling their emotions, they often react with intense joy and gratitude if their partner does even the smallest kind thing for them. The flip side of this is that criticizing a partner with BPD can result in intense anger and hurt. As we have learned, people who suffer from BPD can be very sensitive to the way others treat them and even the smallest criticism can cause them immense amounts of hurt. Sufferers of BPD will experience often violent mood swings, which can be difficult to anticipate. Recognize that this is a symptom of the disorder, and likely not directly related to something you may or may not have done.

Sufferers of BPD fear abandonment and rejection, and this is never more heightened than in a romantic relationship. Experiencing even the smallest amount of conflict can lead your partner to believe that you are about to leave them. Sometimes, in order to avoid this rejection, they will pre-emptively end the relationship in order to be the one to do the "abandoning." Sufferers of BPD will have to work harder than normal to allow themselves to trust their partner and believe that they are not going to leave them.

You have probably noticed your partner tends to pick fights with you when things seem to be going well. People with BPD have often grown up surrounded by such trauma that peace and harmony in a relationship are completely foreign. In order to regain a sense of normalcy, they will seek to uproot this security through aggression, hostility and other damaging behavior. Peace and harmony can actually leave someone with BPD feeling empty and numb. In order to make themselves feel alive, they may attack you, or create conflict in another way. This helps them feel something, which, in their eyes, is better than feeling empty.

In addition, the BPD sufferer's propensity towards black and white thinking means they will often see you as either all good or all bad, often alternating rapidly between intense love and admiration to a crushing dislike and disappointment.

How to Cope

The unpredictability of being a relationship with someone with BPD can cause you to have doubts about your own. It may feel as though the more you love your partner, the less they seem to love you. All this conflict and confusion may have you doubting whether you have the strength to maintain the relationship. These concerns can be heightened by the fact that you don't have your partner to rely on or confide in. This can leave you feeling lost and alone. Implementing the following solutions can make living with BPD much more manageable:

- Get information. Learn as much as you can about what it is like to suffer from BPD. This will help increase empathy in the relationship, and help you understand the struggles faced by your partner on a daily basis. By familiarizing yourself with the traits of the disorder, it should become clear to you that your partner's challenging behavior is the result of an illness, rather than a choice.

- See a counselor. Seeking support from a mental health professional can be invaluable to both sufferers of BPD and their loved ones. You may choose to attend therapy sessions alone or as a couple.

- Communicate. Communication is vital in any relationship, but when a partner suffers from BPD, learning how to effectively communicate is of utmost importance. It is crucial however that you take care not to say anything that your partner may perceive as a slight, or may make them feel unloved, or as though the relationship is about to end. Ensure that all discussions you have come from a place of love, rather than attacking your partner or seeking to put them down.

- Ensure your meaning is clear. BPD can cause sufferers to misconstrue what others are saying to them. For this reason, it is important to make sure you communicate your meaning as effectively as possible. Do not assume your facial expression is enough to convey what you are thinking.

- Hold discussions only when your partner is calm. Avoid raising important issues with your partner when they are suffering from an episode of BPD, such as exhibiting mood swings. When faced with decision-making in such a state, a BPD sufferer is likely to act rashly, without thinking about the issues through. They are also more likely to be defensive or aggressive and may turn to self-deprecating or self-harming behaviors in order to help them cope.

- Offer support. We all need support from our loved ones from time to time, and BPD sufferers are no different. Make sure your partner knows you are there for them, in good times and bad.

- Foster a sense of independence in your partner. As we know, BPD can lead a person to greatly fear rejection. Even the smallest of separations such as a vacation or work trip can be a source of immense stress. But these separations can be beneficial for fostering a sense of independence in your partner. Make sure you have parts of your lives that are independent from each other; your own hobbies and circles of friends. While of course, it is wonderful to have a partner with whom you can share so much of your life, having separate interests is great for your partner's sense of independence. If you are apart for longer than a few hours, it can be helpful to check in on your partner, to ensure they understand that the separation is only temporary and that they are not being rejected.

- Avoid blaming everything on their mental illness. Remember that your partner's BPD does not define them. Avoid linking every part of their behavior to the BPD. After all, it is just one facet of who they are. Doing so can cause the disorder to become something of a put-down. See past the illness to your partner's personality and avoid labeling.

- Take threats of self-harm seriously. Threats of self-injury or suicide should always be taken seriously with a partner suffering from BPD. If your partner begins to exhibit signs of self-harming or suicidal behavior, call their therapist or your local suicide prevention helpline.

- Practice self-care. Living with a partner with BPD can be an enormous challenge. It is important to allow yourself time to step back and relax. Ensure you have your own support network in place; people you can rely on if the stress becomes overwhelming. Prioritize time for friends and hobbies, both alone and with your partner.

Conclusion

We've now reached the end of the book and the hope is that you're feeling more positive and motivated to do something about the situation you may find yourself in.

There is no place in a loving relationship for manipulation of any kind. Far too many people stay in manipulative and abusive relationships out of fear of the future, but the future can only be brighter than the present day. Staying in this type of relationship will turn you into a shell of the person you were before. Breaking free will allow you to return to that person, but with an added element of strength and fearlessness.

This book has talked in-depth about everything to do with psychological and emotional manipulation. We've covered a lot of ground, but the content will always be there if you need to go back over anything and refresh your memory.

To an outsider looking in, a manipulative relationship is cut and dried. You walk away because you're not being treated correctly. For the person in the middle of the relationship, it's never that easy. Emotions are involved, thoughts and perceptions are twisted, control is exerted, and confidence is shattered. All of this happens over time, and the slow drip of manipulation is one of the most effective methods of control there are.

There isn't one particular type of person who is more likely to be more vulnerable to manipulation than another, but narcissists are very good at identifying people who may be a little lacking in confidence or going through an especially hard time. Those people may be more vulnerable in some ways, but that doesn't mean that a person who seems very strong and confident on the outside can't be subjected to manipulation too.

If there is one message we want you to take away from this book, it's that any type of manipulation is wrong. Even if the manipulation is from a narcissist who has a specific personality disorder, none of this is an excuse. Treating other people with no care, thought, or emotion is always something that should never be tolerated. Finding the strength to walk away will be the best thing you ever do.

Of course, it could be that you are watching a close friend or family live their lives under the clutches of a manipulative partner. We hope that this book has educated you on what that person might be going through and feeling. As a result, you're in a much better position to help them deal with the situation and hopefully break free from it in time.

Narcissism is difficult to explain to someone who has never been affected by it. This is a personality disorder that may cause extreme distress to other people, but at the heart of it all, the narcissist isn't happy either. All you can do in any situation is look after yourself, and that means breaking free, looking to the future, and finding a situation that makes you happy, free from manipulation of any sort.

As we bid you goodbye, we won't wish you good luck, we will wish you strength instead.

www.ingramcontent.com/pod-product-compliance
Lightning Source LLC
Chambersburg PA
CBHW070715250726
48662CB00001B/432